THE NICHE OF LIGHTS

Al-Ghazālī

The Niche of Lights

مشكاة الأنوار

A parallel English–Arabic text
translated, introduced, and annotated by

David Buchman

Brigham Young University Press ✦ Provo, Utah

LIBRARY OF CONGRESS CATALOGING-IN-PUBLICATION DATA

Ghazzali, 1058–1111.
[Mishkat al-anwar. English and Arabic]
The niche of lights = Mishkat al-anwar / al-Ghazali:
a parallel English-Arabic text translated, introduced, and annotated
by David Buchman. — 1st ed.
p. cm.— (Islamic translation series)
Includes bibliographical references and index.
ISBN 0-8425-2353-7 (cloth)
1. Sufism—Doctrines—Early works to 1800. 2. Koran. Surat
al-nur, 35—Criticism, interpretation, etc. I. Buchman, David, 1964– .
II. Title. III. Title: Mishkat al-anwar. IV. Series.
BP189.26.G3913 1998
297.4'1—dc21 98-25466
CIP

PRINTED IN THE UNITED STATES OF AMERICA.

2 3 4 5 6 7 8 9 07 06 05 04 03 02 01 00

Contents

The Second Chapter

The Third Chapter

Foreword to the Series

The Islamic Translation Series: Philosophy, Theology, and Mysticism (hereafter ITS) is designed not only to further scholarship in Islamic studies but, by encouraging the translation of Islamic texts into the technical language of contemporary Western scholarship, to assist in the integration of Islamic studies into Western academia and to promote global perspectives in the disciplines to which it is devoted. If this goal is achieved, it will not be for the first time: Historians well know that, during the so-called Middle Ages, a portion of the philosophical, scientific, and mathematical wealth of the Islamic tradition entered into and greatly enriched the West. Even Christian theology was affected, as is brilliantly evidenced in the works of St. Thomas Aquinas and other scholastics.

Manuscripts submitted to ITS for consideration are, of course, evaluated without regard to the religious, methodological, or political preferences of the translators or to their gender or national origins. The translator of each text, not the editors of the series nor the members of the advisory board, is solely responsible for the volume in question.

On behalf of Daniel C. Peterson, the managing editor, and members of the advisory board, I wish to express deep appreciation to the cosponsoring institutions for their gracious support of this project. Special thanks are due to the Center for the Preservation of Ancient Religious Texts of Brigham Young University and to the Institute of Global Cultural Studies of Binghamton University and its director, Ali A. Mazrui.

—Parviz Morewedge
Editor-in-Chief
Binghamton, New York

◆ ◆ ◆

Brigham Young University and its Center for the Preservation of Ancient Religious Texts are pleased to sponsor and publish the Islamic Translation Series: Philosophy, Theology, and Mysticism (ITS). We wish to express our appreciation to the editor-in-chief of ITS, Parviz Morewedge, for joining us in this important project. We are especially grateful to James L. and Beverley Sorenson of Salt Lake City for their generous support, which made ITS possible, and to the Ashton Family Foundation of Orem, Utah, which kindly provided additional funding so that we might continue.

Islamic civilization represents nearly fourteen centuries of intense intellectual activity, and believers in Islam number in the hundreds of millions. The texts that will appear in the ITS are among the treasures of this great culture. But they are more than that. They are properly the inheritance of all the peoples of the world. As an institution of The Church of Jesus Christ of Latter-day Saints, Brigham Young University is honored to assist in making these texts available to many for the first time. In doing so, we hope to serve our fellow human beings, of all creeds and cultures. We also follow the admonition of our own tradition, to "seek . . . out of the best books words of wisdom," believing, indeed, that "the glory of God is intelligence."

—Daniel C. Peterson
Managing Editor
Brigham Young University

Foreword

Al-Ghazālī needs no introduction to those familiar with Islamic studies; and for those not familiar, David Buchman has summarized the scholarly research in the introduction to his translation. Perhaps I can say something useful about the importance of *The Niche of Lights (Mishkāt al-anwār)* in the development of Islamic "theology" in the broadest sense of the term.

If we look at Islamic teachings as addressing three basic domains of human experience—doing, knowing, and being; or practice, doctrine, and realization; or *islām, īmān,* and *iḥsān*—then Ṣūfism focuses specifically on the last, employing the first and the second, however, as its primary means to achieve this focus. The great authorities who spoke for Ṣūfism were thoroughly learned in all three domains, while authorities in other domains tended to limit themselves to their own expertise. The jurists, *qua* jurists, claimed to be experts only in proper activity, while the authorities of *kalām* investigated correct understanding of the articles of faith. Al-Ghazālī, among others, was interested in all three domains of learning and wrote specialized treatises in the first two as well as works that integrated all three. His great *Iḥyā᾽ ᶜulūm al-dīn* is a grand example of a work that harmonizes these three modes of participating in the Islamic revelation. Perhaps his greatest contribution here was to make it indisputable among the *ᶜulamā᾽* that the third and innermost domain, *iḥsān,* is an inherent and essential part of Islam. If we call this third domain of Islamic learning "Ṣūfism," we will be following the example of many Ṣūfī authorities; but, given the fact that the word Ṣūfism means different things to different people, it is perhaps best not to waste too much time disputing with those who want to say that "al-Ghazālī was not a Ṣūfī" or that "Ṣūfism has nothing to do with Islam."

Early texts that deal with Islam's third dimension tend to focus on the human qualities that need to be achieved if one is to gain proximity to God. These qualities, sometimes called the "stations" *(maqāmāt)* on the path to God, usually impinge directly on morality and ethics; but the discussions do not have a moralistic tone. What such works address has rightly been called "spiritual psychology," and it involves describing the perfections of the human soul and the means to achieve these perfections through one's interactions with God and other human beings.

The earliest works on what might be called Ṣūfī "doctrine," such as al-Kalābādhī's *al-Taᶜarruf li madhhab al-taṣawwuf* (translated by Arberry as *The Doctrine of the Ṣūfīs*), are informed by arguments that fit well into the context of *kalām*. The approach is one of providing rational interpretations of Qurᵓānic verses in the manner of the theologians, but in this case the authors are attempting to prove that the practices and "stations" of the Ṣūfīs are fully Islamic. Such works are very different in standpoint from those of Ibn al-ᶜArabī, who marks the full flowering of the theoretical exposition of Ṣūfī teachings and who addresses in extraordinary detail all the implications of the Qurᵓānic teachings for the three domains of Islamic learning. From his time onward, many Ṣūfī authors devote most of their attention to explicating the articles of faith, which are the same basic topics studied by the theologians and the philosophers—God, the angels, the books, the prophets, the last day, and the "measuring out" *(qadar)*, both the good of it and the evil of it. What differentiated Ṣūfī writings from those of the philosophers and theologians was the point of view and the epistemological premises.

The Ṣūfīs strove to achieve perfect *iḥsān*, which involved, according to the Prophet's definition, "worshipping God as if you see Him." From the point of view of this "as if," the world appears as a far different place than from the point of view of jurisprudence, whose characteristic stance in relation to God is "we hear and we obey," with no talk of seeing. Both *kalām* and most of Islamic philosophy accepted that there was nothing of God to be seen in this world, but that God could be thought about. The tool for thinking about God is *ᶜaql*—reason, or the rational faculty. What these two disciplines share is a basic trust in the ability of human reason to explain the human relationship to God in more or less adequate terms. It is here that most of the Ṣūfīs disagreed; and their theoretical elaborations of the domain of faith stressed precisely that God must also be understood, not by thinking about Him, but "as if" we see Him.

When reason is left to its own devices, it recognizes at best a God who is infinitely distant and difficult of access. Ṣūfīs accepted this point of view, but they insisted that it had to be complemented by another point of view, according to which God is "with you wherever you are," as the Qurᵓān puts it. Presence, in short, is just as important as absence; the divine immanence is every bit as real as the divine transcendence. In the terminology of Ibn al-ᶜArabī's school, God's similarity *(tashbīh)* must be conceded if we are to understand the true significance of declaring Him incomparable *(tanzīh)*. For Ibn al-ᶜArabī and his followers, grasping God's similarity demands a full appreciation and understanding of the "as if," and this can only come through imagination *(khayāl)*. If reason sees things in the abstract and understands God as different and other, imagination grasps the concrete and recognizes God as same and self. In other words, imagination sees God in the image. It recognizes everything in the universe as a "symbol" of God—not in the sense that one thing points to another thing, but in the sense that God is actually present in the things, just as He is actually absent from them.

What al-Ghazālī does in *Mishkāt al-anwār,* in a more systematic and focused manner than in his other writings, is to bring out the importance of the imaginal dimension of reality for a proper perception of the relationship between God and the world. It is not enough to abstract God from the world in the manner of the theologians; one must also perceive His presence. The Qurᵓān often refers to its teachings about God by employing the words *mathal* and *mithāl,* "similitude" and "likeness," so it is not surprising to see that al-Ghazālī pays a good deal of attention to explaining the true Qurᵓānic sense of these words. Certainly he is striving, among other things, to show that the "symbolism" of the Qurᵓān should not be thought of primarily as literary imagery, as similes and metaphors. On the contrary, God employs the language that He employs to clarify the actual nature of reality. At issue are the structure of the cosmos and the human soul.

I am sure that many people will share my delight that David Buchman has provided us with a long-overdue, accurate English translation of this classic work.

—William C. Chittick
Mt. Sinai, New York

Acknowledgments

This translation project culminates ten years of studies under the guidance of Drs. William C. Chittick and Sachiko Murata. Their extraordinary patience in teaching is surpassed only by their knowledge of Islam and concern for their students. Much of my understanding and knowledge of Islam and Ṣūfism come from their classes, books, and discussions. Like many other students and scholars of Islamic studies, I have greatly benefited from them and continue to do so. I owe special gratitude to Dr. Chittick, who first suggested that I translate this text and who carefully oversaw the work each step of the way. Nevertheless, all errors remain mine. I would also like to thank Dr. W. Arens, my advisor in anthropology, who, seeing the relevance of textual studies to the anthropological study of Islam, made it possible for me to complete this project during graduate coursework. Finally, I would like to thank Elizabeth Watkins and D. Morgan Davis for the excellent and meticulous editing and critical comments that improved the final version of this translation, making it a clearer and more readable English text.

—David Buchman
New York, May 1998

Translator's Introduction

The exact date when Abū Ḥamid al-Ghazālī (1058–1111) wrote *The Niche of Lights (Mishkāt al-anwār)* is not known. However, the nature of the book and the fact that al-Ghazālī mentions other dated works have led scholars to suppose that the treatise was composed toward the end of his life, after he had written his magnum opus, *The Revivification of the Religious Sciences (Iḥyāʾ ʿulūm al-dīn)*.[1]

Al-Ghazālī says that he wrote the book for a friend who requested from him the "mysteries of the divine lights, along with an interpretation of the apparent meanings of" Qurʾānic verses and *ḥadīth* (sayings and actions of the Prophet Muḥammad) that allude to these lights (p. 1). Although the Qurʾān and *ḥadīth* are incorporated into the book's argument, it is organized around an explanation of the well-known Light Verse (*āyat al-nūr*, Qurʾān 24:35) and a *ḥadīth* related thematically to this verse, sometimes called the "Veils *Ḥadīth*."[2] The book's title is derived from the Light Verse, which reads:

> God is the light of the heavens and the earth; the likeness of His light is as a niche wherein is a lamp, the lamp in a glass, the glass as it were a glittering star kindled from a blessed tree, an olive that is neither of the East nor of the West, whose oil well-nigh would shine, even if no fire touched it; light upon light; God guides to His light whom He will. And God strikes similitudes for men, and God has knowledge of everything.

The Veils *Ḥadīth* reads as follows:

> God has seventy veils of light and darkness; were He to lift them, the august glories of His face would burn up everyone whose eyesight perceived Him.

The most outstanding characteristic of al-Ghazālī's exegesis of these passages is that he explains their meaning by establishing a metaphysics of light—which includes an ontology and an epistemology—and interrelated cosmological and psychological schemes based upon this metaphysics. Moreover, he does so from within a Ṣūfī perspective[3] that played an important role in how he came to live and conceive of Islam in the second half of his life.

The text speaks to anyone desiring knowledge of God, the universe, humanity, and how they interrelate. Al-Ghazālī presents these themes in a brief and unpretentious manner, using highly evocative and easily understood metaphors and similes. The book avoids dry and abstract theological jargon. It paints a picture of the world and the human being with concrete imagery immediately recognizable and applicable to everyday experiences. Although *The Niche of Lights* is over eight hundred years old, its language and ideas are timeless, appealing to all those who look for insights into the relationship between God and the cosmos. But the text is also thoroughly grounded in Qurʾānic imagery and teachings, and especially the cardinal principle of *tawḥīd,* the declaration that God is One. While the book could stand by itself with little or no introduction, it may be helpful to elucidate the general "*tawḥīd*-centered" worldview of twelfth-century Islam. People today—Muslims and non-Muslims alike—usually hold drastically different assumptions on the nature of existence than those held by al-Ghazālī and most of his contemporaries. Knowing the tacit but prevalent presuppositions of the medieval Muslim *Weltanschauung* enables the contemporary reader to understand the depth and beauty of al-Ghazālī's interpretation of divine unity.

The Niche of Lights as a Ṣūfī work

Islam's faith and practice are based on interpretations of the Qurʾān and *ḥadīth.* The Qurʾān—from the Arabic word meaning "recitation"—is a book in Arabic that Muslims believe is the literal word of God given to the Prophet Muḥammad through the intermediary of the archangel Gabriel. *Ḥadīth*—the Arabic word meaning "news," "a tale," "a story," or "report"—are the recorded sayings and actions of Muḥammad, whom Muslims consider the preeminent interpreter of the Qurʾān.[4]

Throughout Islamic history, certain people have arisen who have produced such well-respected interpretations of these sacred texts that they have become enduring touchstones of piety and practice. Many Muslims have deemed al-Ghazālī such a person. Several of his writings have been considered among the most important interpretive sources of Islamic faith and practice down to modern times.[5] During his own lifetime he was known as "the Proof of Islam" *(ḥujjat al-islām)* and "the Renewer of the Religion" *(mujaddid al-dīn)*.[6] Such lofty praise has encouraged Western scholars to produce abundant critical literature on his life and ideas.[7]

One reason al-Ghazālī was given such titles by his contemporaries was the nature of his contributions to Islamic thought. By the time he was thirty-four, he had excelled in almost every sphere of Muslim scholarship. He was known not only as the leading jurist *(faqīh)* and dogmatic theologian *(mutakallim)* of his day but as the clearest expositor and religious opponent of Islamic Peripatetic philosophy. His extant writings on these subjects are *loci classici* for Muslims around the world.[8]

The treatises that al-Ghazālī composed in the first part of his life criticized and refined the rational methods employed by the jurists, theologians, and philosophers in their search for knowledge of God.[9] They do not explain the inner dimension of Islamic teachings or describe how to cultivate the sincere intentions and virtuous attitudes that should accompany religiously guided behavior. They neither emphasize the need for a Muslim to become near to God in this life nor recognize the notion that divine knowledge can be actualized directly within the heart—the center of one's being.

Islamic jurisprudence *(sharīʿa)* is considered by Muslims to be a revealed law that determines the behavior God requires from human beings. It is derived from the interpretation of divine knowledge revealed in the Qurʾān and *ḥadīth*. This law establishes how Muslims must worship God *(ʿibāda)* and, in addition, sets principles and standards determining all human familial, social, political, and economic interactions *(muʿāmalāt)*. Law teaches how one should behave in a manner pleasing to God in this life so as to enter Paradise in the next; it is not directly concerned with how to think about divinity, the afterlife, and the unseen *(ghayb)* world. Jurisprudence explains the behavior necessary to *do* good; it does not teach the virtuous attitudes of *being* good.

Islam produced other schools of thought to fill the spiritual, intellectual, and emotional needs of people that jurisprudence could not satisfy. The schools of theology, philosophy *(falsafa)*, and theoretical Ṣūfism *(taṣawwuf)* explain the meaning of the law, the virtues necessary for its efficacy, and ideas that provide the intellectual justification for adhering to it. Such schools developed ways to think about the contents of faith (that is, God, His angels, books, messengers, the Day of Judgment, and the idea that He measures everything out, both good and evil), providing the worldviews in which to practice the divine law.

All these schools used rational explanations to elucidate the nature of God as He reveals Himself through revelation and the universe. However, the methods of their rational inquiry differed. The theologian gained knowledge of God through rational analysis of the Qur᾽ān and *ḥadīth.* For example, both texts mention that God has names and attributes. One theological discussion dealt with the nature of these names as intermediary between God and the world: God created the world through acts *(afᶜāl)* that manifest his names. Philosophers, while practicing Muslims, did not usually turn to the Qur᾽ān and *ḥadīth* for knowledge of God. The rational faculty *(ᶜaql)* of the human mind, they argued, has the ability to know the divine through proper observation and reflection upon the universe without the need for revealed books. They believed that a purified *ᶜaql* could attain the greatest knowledge of God and that such cognition would not contradict the basic teachings of revelation.

As al-Ghazālī argues in *The Niche of Lights,* there is a knowledge of God that goes beyond the rational ability to know Him and is "unveiled" *(kashf)* by God in the heart. Jurisprudence, theology, and philosophy are not directly concerned with how to actualize this direct God-given knowledge; their interest lies in knowledge acquired through reason. Inner knowledge of God is a divine gift usually bestowed only after one has struggled to purify one's inner reality, the soul, from everything other than God, thereby realizing a type of divine proximity.

The practices of Ṣūfism are aimed at cleansing the soul from the dross of ignorance and egoistic tendencies. In contrast, theoretical Ṣūfism offers rational discussions on the nature of God, the world, and the human being. An important function of this discourse is to provide worldviews congruent with the supererogatory rituals undertaken by Muslims following practical Ṣūfism. The core focus of Ṣūfism in practice centers around becoming a disciple and following the religious guidance of a Ṣūfī master *(shaykh).* One of the desired consequences of such endeavors is that God should bestow on the disciple knowledge directly from Him. This knowledge is seen as more pure and intimate than the ideas of God acquired by the rational faculty from outside sources, such as God's revealed books or study of the cosmos.

In the second part of al-Ghazālī's life, after achieving mastery over law, theology, and philosophy, he began following Ṣūfism seriously, writing books that combined the teachings of law and theology/philosophy with ideas explaining the necessity of cleansing the soul.[10] Such texts brought out the inner aspect of Muslim teachings and showed the necessity of cultivating beauty, goodness, and sincerity in religion so as to attain nearness to God in this life. His linguistic style remained academic, but his ideas were now directed toward the scholar and layperson alike. Due to the universality of the concerns of these later writings, they came to surpass his earlier scholarship in influence and fame in the Islamic world. *The Niche of Lights* is among the works written in the last part of al-Ghazālī's life and combines all three aspects of Islamic teachings—law, theology/philosophy, and purification of the human heart from everything other than the remembrance *(dhikr)* of God.

Al-Ghazālī's life and work

Al-Ghazālī was born in the small city of Ṭūṣ in what is now northeastern Iran. His father died when he was young, but left enough money for his education and that of his brother Aḥmad.[11] Abū Ḥamid was an exceptionally bright student and showed his gift through his quick progress in the study of jurisprudence *(fiqh)* and dogmatic theology *(kalām)*. The Ashᶜarite theology that he learned consisted of dry discussions limited to defending certain contents of Islamic faith using simple logic. It subordinated reason to revelation, thus viewing rationality as incapable of explaining the divine word.[12] At the same time, theology used rational thought to defend faith.[13]

During his twenties, al-Ghazālī went to the city of Nishapur to study under the leading theologian of the day, al-Juwaynī (d. 1085).[14] After al-Juwaynī's death, al-Ghazālī began writing texts on Islamic law and theology that are still used today as standard source books for the instruction of these subjects in traditional Islamic colleges *(madāris)*.[15]

After completing his formal studies, al-Ghazālī left Nishapur for the political "camp" of Niẓām al-Mulk, the vizier of the Seljuk king Malikshāh. At that time, Egypt was ruled by the Fāṭimids, who followed the Ismāᶜīlī branch of Shīᶜism and promoted a religious doctrine denounced as Bāṭinite by its detractors. Bāṭinite (from the Arabic adjectival noun *bāṭinīya*) was "a name given to (a) the Ismāᶜīlīs in medieval times, referring to their stress on the *bāṭin*, the 'inward' meaning behind the literal wording of sacred texts; and (b), less specifically, to anyone accused of rejecting the literal meaning of such texts in favour of the *bāṭin*."[16]

The Fāṭimids used their religious doctrines to aid in achieving political hegemony and were sending secret envoys into the ᶜAbbāsid territory. These envoys attempted to convert people to Ismāᶜīlism, which in turn would imply political allegiance to the Fāṭimids. Niẓām al-Mulk, seeing al-Ghazālī's rhetorical genius and keen intellect, had him write political-religious treatises against the Bāṭinite doctrine. For al-Ghazālī, however, these works were more than simply politically motivated, since they were grounded in what he felt to be a defense of a correct religious teaching. His *Niche of Lights,* written perhaps twenty years later, contains an interpretation of the Bāṭinite belief system and explains why al-Ghazālī felt it to be a one-sided understanding of Islamic principles.[17]

After spending time with Niẓām al-Mulk, al-Ghazālī, then only thirty-four, was assigned to the highest educational post in the ᶜAbbāsid empire. He was made rector and professor of the Niẓāmiya *madrasa* in Baghdād, at that time one of the major learning centers for Islamic law and theology. During his rectorship at the Niẓāmiya college, al-Ghazālī wrote his well-known book on Peripatetic philosophy, *The Intentions of the Philosophers (Maqāṣid al-falāsifa),* in which he summarized the theories of al-Kindī, al-Fārābī, and Ibn Sīnā (Avicenna). The work was so clear and presented such a knowledgeable summary of Peripatetic philosophy that, when it was made available in Latin translation to the Christian scholastics, "Albert the Great (d. 1280), Thomas Aquinas (d. 1274), and Roger Bacon (d. 1294) all repeatedly mentioned the name of the author of the 'Intentions of the Philosophers' along with Ibn Sīnā and Ibn Rushd (Averroës, d. 1198) as the true representatives of Arab Aristotelianism."[18]

Al-Ghazālī wrote *The Intentions* to prepare the ground for a second book called *The Incoherence of the Philosophers (Tahāfut al-falāsifa).*[19] In *The Intentions* he clearly laid out the principles of philosophy, showing what it could and could not know. In *The Incoherence* he then directed a critical attack upon certain philosophic positions—an attack that led to a decline of Peripatetic philosophy. Peripateticism was revived in the western lands of Islam a generation later by Ibn Rushd, who answered al-Ghazālī's attack in his *The Incoherence of the Incoherence (Tahāfut al-tahāfut).* In the eastern lands, Peripatetic philosophy was gradually harmonized with other philosophical teachings that emphasized the role of inner knowledge of God gained through illumination and "unveiling," or mystical intuition.[20]

ᶜAfīfī argues that *The Niche* influenced the Illuminationist *(ishrāqī)* philosophy of Suhrawardī al-Maqtūl and his followers. He maintains that, while it is not a philosophical text, it is nevertheless one of the earliest treatises to equate—in a systematic manner—knowledge of God with the illumination of the heart by the Divine Light. He claims that *The Niche* might have inspired such great Illuminationist philosophers as Suhrawardī and Mullā Ṣadrā.[21] If he is correct, then al-Ghazālī's effect on Islamic philosophy was not just destructive but also formative.

One of al-Ghazālī's major criticisms of the Peripatetic thought of Ibn Sīnā and al-Fārābī focused on knowledge of God through revelation. Al-Ghazālī divided philosophy into the study of mathematics, logic, physics, politics, ethics, and metaphysics. He had no complaint with mathematics, logic, and physics and no major criticism of politics and ethics, but he was dismayed at the philosophers' logical incoherence in metaphysical speculation. In his view, metaphysics concerned the unseen reality of God and His relation to the universe, which are clearly enunciated in the Qur'ān and *ḥadīth.* In *The Incoherence* he attempted to show that philosophy can neither prove nor disprove the truth of religion and that the effort to do so made the philosophers themselves take positions that are nonsensical.[22]

After the completion of *The Incoherence,* al-Ghazālī experienced a profound crisis, including a complete physical breakdown. In his autobiographical account of his search for knowledge of God, *Al-munqidh min al-ḍalāl,* he admits that he came to understand the necessity of the inward journey to God. He now understood that knowledge of God entails more than just rational speculation. It also means to realize His presence in the heart, which is the center of one's inward reality or soul.[23] This purification process occurs through "journeying" *(sulūk)* on the "path" *(ṭarīqa)* to God. With each successive stage of purification, the heart's awareness of the divine increases and one becomes "closer" to God.

Al-Ghazālī saw that the study of divine law, dogmatic theology, and philosophy are beneficial only when combined with inward striving for divine proximity. What makes his recognition of this special is that he had immersed himself in all three ways of knowing God—law, theology, and philosophy—and had surpassed the greatest of Islamic thinkers in all three fields. He was to conclude that to be human means not just to follow religion with the body and mind but to try to transform the soul through the practices of Ṣūfism.

Recent scholarship on Ṣūfī literature points out that Ṣūfī practices and teachings are not, as one might conclude from much of the early Western scholarship, secondary "mystical" and/or antinomian teachings added as a kind of afterthought to basic Muslim religiosity. According to the well-known writers on this subject, such as al-Ghazālī, Ṣūfism is the core or essence of Islamic teachings. It functions within Islam to enliven and give depth of meaning to Muslim belief and ritual.[24]

For al-Ghazālī, as for other Ṣūfīs, the purifying work of Ṣūfism begins with the meticulous practice of the *sharīʿa.* Following the divine law with correct intentions and as a foundation for life polishes the soul. However, other devotional practices are necessary for inner transformation. These "supererogatory" acts are accomplished under the guidance of a Ṣūfī master. The most important of these acts is *dhikr,* the constant mentioning and remembrance of a revealed divine name or formula. Since *dhikr,* like the *sharīʿa,* perfects the soul and makes it beautiful, the disciple strives to achieve the ceaseless repetition of God's name in the heart.[25]

The human manifestation of a pure heart is to act in a beautiful manner *(iḥsān)* and with virtue *(faḍāʾil).* Classical Ṣūfī literature has been devoted from the beginning to understanding the meaning of the virtues and realizing how their cultivation is an essential aspect of spiritual development. Hence, in addition to teaching the *dhikr,* the master instills in the student the importance of cultivating virtuous attitudes such as generosity, patience, humility, God-fearingness, vigilance, and many others. The means of achieving these attitudes was the main theme of many Ṣūfī manuals.[26] Al-Ghazālī maintains that when the *dhikr* and *sharīʿa* are practiced with understanding and in a sincere and upright manner, the soul becomes beautiful, perfect, and worthy of approaching God's presence.

In his autobiography, al-Ghazālī explains that he studied the various sciences including jurisprudence, theology, and philosophy. Then he writes,

> When I finished with all those kinds of lore, I brought my mind to bear on the way of the Ṣūfīs. I knew that their particular Way is consummated [realized] only by knowledge and by activity [by the union of theory and practice]. The aim of their knowledge is to lop off the obstacles present in the soul and to rid oneself of its reprehensible habits and vicious qualities in order to attain thereby a heart empty of all save God and adorned with the constant remembrance [*dhikr*] of God.[27]

The knowledge of God afforded by theology, philosophy, and law is based upon the rational interpretation of the divine wisdom found in the Qurʾān and *ḥadīth.* This type of knowledge is gained and perfected through the rational faculty of the mind; its acquisition is not directly dependent upon the morality and inner goodness of a person. Al-Ghazālī perceived that he could excel in rational knowledge while remaining egotistical and arrogant.

Ṣūfism demands the whole person—not just the mental manipulation of ideas. The knowledge of God that Ṣūfī discipline imparts is dependent on the quality of a person's being—or, in Islamic terminology, the state of an individual's soul. That is why al-Ghazālī says of Ṣūfism in the above quote, "I knew that their particular Way is realized only by knowledge and by activity." Only a person with a pure and beautiful heart—the soul's center—can become aware of God's presence and obtain direct knowledge from Him. Only someone sincere in religion, whose soul is made praiseworthy through the ornaments of virtue, is capable of attaining divine nearness and knowledge. People whose inner reality is impure may become masters of the sciences of law, theology, and philosophy, but they never actualize the wisdom offered through the sincere practice of Islam demanded by Ṣūfism.

Al-Ghazālī's crisis began when he realized that in order for him to be sincere in Islam he must change his life. He knew that the journey to God entailed ridding oneself of the obstacles of "reprehensible habits and vicious qualities" that, for him, stemmed from his attachment to his current lifestyle. He could not easily give up his reputation, fortune, family, children, and associates for the sake of the journey to God. Nevertheless, he saw the necessity of doing so. For six months he was pulled in two directions; he could either stay where he was, with the knowledge that his actions and teaching of Islamic law and theology were hypocritical and, if left alone, would lead him to the fires of hell; or he could leave his job, relatives, and friends, find an appropriate Ṣūfī master, and begin the arduous task of purifying his soul. He writes,

> In the morning I would have a sincere desire to seek the things of the afterlife; but by the evening the host of passion would assault and render it lukewarm. Mundane desires began tugging me with their chains to remain as I was, while the herald of faith was crying out: "Away! Up and away! Only a little is left of your life, and a long journey lies before you! All the theory and practice in which you are engrossed is eye service and fakery! If you do not prepare now for the afterlife, when will you do so? And if you do not sever these attachments now, then when will you sever them?"[28]

The rational knowledge gained from study did not purify his soul of everything other than God. While his outward behavior was guided by the divine law, his inward intentions were attached to the celebrity and glory he had achieved in the world. In this state, al-Ghazālī knew that his soul was repulsive, base, and far from God's knowledge and beauty.

Under the pretense of going on the pilgrimage *(ḥajj)* to Mecca, al-Ghazālī gave up his teaching post and for ten years practiced and studied Ṣūfism under masters of the *ṭarīqa.* He lived in Damascus, Mecca, and Medina, and eventually returned to the town of his birth, Ṭūṣ. After this period of spiritual struggle, al-Ghazālī used the knowledge he had of law, theology, and philosophy along with his own experiences of the path to God to write the work that became the classic manual on the meaning of Islamic practice: *The Revivification of the Religious Sciences.*

The well-known *Revivification* is a lengthy work consisting of four volumes containing ten books each. Though al-Ghazālī uses his theological and philosophical training in the book's rhetorical style, it is not a treatise on theology or philosophy. Rather, it deals with practical morality and piety and has generally been considered the most authoritative book on the meaning of Islamic practice. It is a handbook on developing and deepening one's attitudes, emotions, and inner comprehension of Islamic law. If Islamic law is only concerned with the correct way of doing things and not with the meaning of activity, and if theology and philosophy are too abstract to be relevant for day-to-day religious life, then *The Revivification* explains in beautiful language and profound detail how law is relevant to the moral and ethical demands of Islamic belief. It accomplishes this by showing the way to increase knowledge of the inner meaning of the law's form. Al-Ghazālī was able to synthesize all the diverse trends of Islamic thought and practice—law, theology, philosophy, and Ṣūfism—into a rhetoric that has been recognized throughout the Muslim world as an outstanding expression of what is Islamic.

Toward the end of al-Ghazālī's life, after ten years away from the public sphere, he returned to teaching. It is said that he would give different advice in keeping with the various needs of his students. He had disciples not only in law and theology, but also in the ascent to God, which he felt contained the only true happiness. To some he would teach law, to others theology, and to others Ṣūfī doctrine and practice.

The story of al-Ghazālī's life is the story of how he came to see that Ṣūfism is an essential dimension of Islam. As a consequence of this self-realization, he saw that Muslim belief and practice were misunderstood by many practitioners, including himself at the early stages of his career. Many people were following Islam hypocritically, without the sincere intention of striving to know and love God in this life. He saw that to revive Islam among people the *sharīʿa* must be infused with the practice of its inner dimension, Ṣūfism. Otherwise, the outward action of the law remained misunderstood by the practitioner and ineffectual for salvation. The Arabic word *muslim* means "one who has submitted." A true Muslim, then, is one who unifies the outward submission to God with the inward submission of the purified soul under the instructions of a Ṣūfī master.

Al-Ghazālī stood apart from most other Muslims who were advanced on the path to God because he had a unique gift to convey in writing the necessity of Ṣūfism to law and of law to Ṣūfism. In *The Revivification of the*

Religious Sciences, he elucidated the inner, or Ṣūfī, dimension of Islam using a rhetoric acceptable to many Muslims who viewed *taṣawwuf* in an unfavorable light. He showed the Muslim jurists the necessity of Ṣūfism for actualizing the sincere practice of the law, while at the same time revealing that antinomian Ṣūfism had no place in Islam.

Studies on *The Niche of Lights*

The Niche of Lights is a smaller and more explicitly Ṣūfī text than *The Revivification* because it presents in straightforward and simple language the message of realizing God's nearness as a human imperative. *The Revivification* clothes this message in long theological, philosophical, and juridical passages more palatable to the tastes of theologians, philosophers, and jurists than that of nonspecialists.

Most prior scholarship on *The Niche* has tended to overlook the significance of the message of attaining nearness to God and its implication in the interpretation of Islam. Earlier literature on this book has centered on the textual authenticity of the third section, speculation on the nature of a certain cosmological reality mentioned in the same section, and the supposed esoteric and Neoplatonic emanationist teachings of al-Ghazālī found in *The Niche* and other works reserved for an elect.

Watt says that the third chapter of the *Mishkāt* is spurious. He argues that this part of the book presents a Neoplatonic conception of the universe and that, based upon al-Ghazālī's previous criticism of such ideas in Peripatetic philosophy, he would never have used Neoplatonism in his discussion; therefore, he concludes, the third section must be a forgery. Along with other factors, Watt uses this same assumed anti-Neoplatonic standard of al-Ghazālī to determine the authenticity of other works assigned to him.[29]

Later scholars such as ʿAfīfī, Davidson, Landolt, and Lazarus-Yafeh find Watt's assertions unconvincing. In answer to Watt's claim that al-Ghazālī was anti-Neoplatonic, Lazarus-Yafeh says instead that al-Ghazālī did use Neoplatonic ideas, but only insofar as those ideas conformed to basic Islamic teachings.[30] Wensinck, who wrote explicitly about the Neoplatonic ideas of the book before Watt, saw the *Mishkāt* as al-Ghazālī's attempt to express his mystical experience of God in a manner "parallel to [Peripatetic] philosophy, yet keeping its [the book's] own position."[31]

While Watt's arguments have been shown to be unreasonable, there is evidence that the third section might have had various forms in the past. Landolt contends that there is evidence from two works of the well-known theologian *(mutakallim)* Fakhr al-Dīn Rāzī that the extant last section might have had two or more versions during the twelfth century.[32] These renditions had different structures. One version was set up to play down Ṣūfī overtones, while the other rendering, as it is found today, was constructed to play up the importance of such teachings. In any event, Landolt does not feel that these variations provide proof of a spurious third section of the *Mishkāt*. He concludes by saying that "only a careful examination of the *whole* manuscript tradition [of *The Niche*], plus external evidence . . . , might eventually cast light on these divergences and show to what extent, if any, they do have a bearing on the authenticity question."[33]

In the last section of the text al-Ghazālī mentions an awesome unseen creature who acts as an intermediary between God's oneness and the multiple worlds of the cosmos, whose rotations are governed by angels. God's single reality is too incomparable to be directly involved with these angels, so an intermediary is necessary. He calls this being *al-muṭāᶜ*, "the one who is obeyed," because the angels move the cosmos by obeying this creature's authority. *Al-muṭāᶜ* itself orders only what God commands. The text does not mention the identity of this being, and this became a point of contention for later critics of al-Ghazālī's teachings, especially for those who saw al-Ghazālī as a hidden follower of the Peripatetic teachings he criticized as incoherent.

Ibn Rushd, motivated to defend Peripatetic philosophy against al-Ghazālī's monumental critique, says in his *Al-kashf ᶜan manāhij al-adilla*[34] that in *The Niche* al-Ghazālī claims that "the one who is obeyed" emanates *(ṣadara)* from God in the sense of the doctrine of emanation supposedly propounded by al-Fārābī and Ibn Sīnā. Hence, in Ibn Rushd's view, al-Ghazālī was two-faced, criticizing the philosophers in *The Incoherence of the Philosophers* and then using their ideas later in *The Niche.* Gairdner shows that al-Ghazālī never employed the technical vocabulary of the doctrine of emanation—terms such as *ṣadara, ṣudūr,* or *fāḍa min.*[35] Lazarus-Yafeh strengthens his argument by saying that al-Ghazālī did use such words as *fāḍa ᶜalā, fayaḍān, faiḍ,* but contextually no emanationist ideas were implied.[36] Hence, in light of al-Ghazālī's vocabulary and usage, Ibn Rushd's accusations are unfounded.[37]

Davidson, in his recent study on the theories of al-Fārābī, Ibn Sīnā, and Ibn Rushd regarding the cosmos and the intellect, agrees with Ibn Rushd's conclusion of al-Ghazālī's duplicity. While al-Ghazālī "avoids stating explicitly that God emanated the universe,"[38] he does imply that emanation occurs among beings of the cosmos. Davidson agrees with

Lazarus-Yafeh that the technical vocabulary of the emanationists was not employed. However, in *The Niche* al-Ghazālī uses emanationist images, such as physical light reflecting from one object to another and water flowing from one thing to another, to describe the way "light"—in certain contexts meaning existence, in others intellect—emanates from one created thing to another.[39] But again, as Lazarus-Yafeh has argued, such ideas did not contradict basic Islamic teachings.[40]

Ibn Ṭufayl, a contemporary of Ibn Rushd, says in his *Ḥayy ibn Yaqẓān* that some later people have misinterpreted al-Ghazālī's discussion of *al-muṭāᶜ*.[41] Gairdner thinks, without certainty, that Ibn Ṭufayl includes Ibn Rushd as one of these "later people." Gairdner explains that Ibn Ṭufayl believed that al-Ghazālī had an esoteric doctrine but that this doctrine did not include the type of emanationism Ibn Rushd believed al-Ghazālī to be promoting. Gairdner maintains that Ibn Ṭufayl did not understand al-Ghazālī's esoteric teachings anyway and that both Ibn Ṭufayl and these "later people," whom Ibn Ṭufayl is criticizing, misread the passage of *The Niche* which forms the basis of their discussions.[42]

While Ibn Rushd and Ibn Ṭufayl were concerned with notions of emanationism in relation to *al-muṭāᶜ*, modern scholars have spent much time attempting to uncover its exact identity. In a personal communication to Gairdner, Louis Massignon suggested that *al-muṭāᶜ* is the pole (*quṭb*)—the human through whom God gives existence to the universe.[43] R. Nicholson equates *al-muṭāᶜ* with the "archetypal Spirit of Muḥammad,"[44] while R. C. Zaehner speculates that this being could be either the angel Gabriel or Muḥammad, though the latter is more likely.[45] Gairdner, and Wensinck after him, say that *al-muṭāᶜ* has nothing to do with a human pole, the Prophet, or the angel Gabriel; instead they identify the creature as the Qurᵓānic Great Spirit (*al-rūḥ;* see 78:38; 97:4).[46] However, Wensinck adds that a human could achieve a type of union with the Spirit in the ascent to God.[47]

Davidson sees no mystery in the identity of this being and finds all this speculation by scholars a bit misplaced.[48] As stated above, he argues that the *Mishkāt* espouses some of Ibn Sīnā's Neoplatonic emanationist ideas. The one of concern here is the notion that the universe consists of, among other things, intellects, intelligences, and souls, some being in charge of the unseen celestial spheres. These realities are created by God but can affect each other through different types of influences that occur in a hierarchical manner from the highest spheres of existence to the lowest. Given this explanation of the cosmos, Davidson says that when al-Ghazālī uses the word *al-muṭāᶜ* he "simply means that the soul of the outermost sphere [of the cosmos] *obeys* the 'command' of the first incorporeal intelligence in the sense that it emulates the intelligence and thereby moves the sphere."[49] Thus, Davidson sees no cryptic message to be deciphered in al-Ghazālī's *al-muṭā*ᶜ.

Along with the notion that al-Ghazālī was at heart a Neoplatonic emanationist of the type he criticized is the contention that he taught such ideas in secret. Hence, there has been lively debate since Ibn Rushd's rebuttal of *The Incoherence of the Philosophers* over the idea that al-Ghazālī held an esoteric doctrine which was Neoplatonic in form and was reserved for an elect audience. Controversy has arisen over certain "discrepancies" found in al-Ghazālī's writings—supposedly he says one thing in one book and then contradicts himself in another. One explanation of these "opposing" positions is that al-Ghazālī's contradictory statements arose from his esoteric doctrine—some works were for an elect, and others were not; hence the "contradiction." Ibn Ṭufayl considered *The Niche* an esoteric book containing doctrines not suitable for the common people.

Lazarus-Yafeh has summarized the various arguments and counter-arguments of the esoteric doctrine debate and concludes that while al-Ghazālī did write differently for different people, he never contradicted himself.[50] Rather, he wrote a single truth, but the form it took varied depending on the abilities of his audience.

> There is no ground for the assumption that Al-Ghazālī has a secret doctrine, which totally contradicted his widely known traditional one. The contradictions between his various books are partly due to the fact that he directed different books to different classes of readers. In books destined for perusal by the "initiated" (such as *"Al-maqsad"* or *"Mishkāt"*) he divulged more of the one and only truth, while in books addressed to the masses he had a more reserved manner. . . . He sometimes made use of both approaches in one and the same volume.[51]

Al-Ghazālī himself admits to levels of a single truth by saying that a person's faith is made up of three layers. The first includes the traditional beliefs acquired from parents and teachers in childhood, which are usually held dear and defended fanatically in debates and discussions. The second layer consists of the instruction and wisdom a teacher imparts to his disciples, to each according to the individual's ability. The final layer is that which one really believes in the inmost heart and which is known to God and oneself only. He may reveal some of these beliefs to those who have reached the same stage of understanding.[52]

Although these issues are interesting for specialists in the history of Islamic thought, this attention to detail has tended to obscure al-Ghazālī's aims in writing *The Niche of Lights:* to outline basic principles of Islamic cosmology and psychology and to demonstrate thereby the human obligation to attain proximity to God through perfecting oneself by sincere practice of Islam.[53]

The text is inspired primarily by the Qur'ān and the *ḥadīth,* and it provides a worldview and conception of the human self compatible with Islamic teachings. What makes it congruent with the message of Islam is not simply that it quotes and employs the terminology of Islam's foundational documents. Rather, it is Qur'ānic because it is based upon the central Muslim principle of *tawḥīd,* the declaration of the unity of God. Hence, although certain ideas in *The Niche of Lights* may be found to parallel Neoplatonic notions, this treatise remains fundamentally Islamic insofar as these notions do not contradict *tawḥīd.*[54]

Al-Ghazālī wrote *The Niche* as an intellectual support for Muslims who want to practice their religion with greater honesty. The text shows, through Islamic cosmological and psychological teachings, that sincere practice demands becoming close to God in this life. As in *The Revivification,* al-Ghazālī asserts that this search for God is only possible through unifying the outer and inner teachings of Islam in faith and practice. But it is important to note that this is not an original idea in Islamic thought. Rather, al-Ghazālī was making explicit the generally understood but sometimes forgotten idea that the central Qur'ānic teaching of *tawḥīd* must be actualized by all Muslims. In *The Niche of Lights,* al-Ghazālī elucidates what was always known in Islam: that purification of the heart, sincerity, and attaining closeness to God are the inevitable interdependent human results of realizing *tawḥīd.*

Tawḥīd is an Arabic noun that literally means "unification and union." It is derived from a verb which means "to make one, to unite, to unify." In Islamic theology it has come to mean "belief in the unity of God; the profession of the unity of God; and monotheism."[55]

The profession of the unity of God is defined by the first half of the testimony of faith, the *shahāda,* which in Arabic is *lā ilāha illā Allāh,* "There is no god but God." The apparent meaning of *tawḥīd* declares that there is only one God, not many gods; and Muslims generally see this idea as the central concept of their faith. Hence, the idea has played a major role in directing the course of any thinking that can properly be called "Islamic," especially theology, philosophy, and the natural and human sciences.[56] Declaring the oneness of God became the metaphysical principle that challenged Muslim thinkers in explaining the significance of anything they studied.

On the level of religious practice *tawḥīd* means that Muslims should declare with their whole reality that God is one. An implicit idea found throughout *The Niche* is that God's oneness demands from the practitioners that they reflect the One by actualizing unity, wholeness, and harmony in their lives. This unifying of self is accomplished physically through following the *sharīʿa* and in one's heart through *dhikr.* In the later half of al-Ghazālī's life, books such as *The Revivification* and *The Niche* revived the religion through making explicit this central teaching of the Qurʾān and *ḥadīth.* Hence, in *The Niche of Lights* we find perhaps the earliest attempt to present theological and philosophical discussions of *tawḥīd* combined with a deep concern for realizing God's unity through the deepening of one's piety and the refinement of one's practice.

The leitmotif of the text is the Qurʾānic notion that God is light.[57] This metaphor provided al-Ghazālī—and later Islamic thinkers—with a powerful means of expressing the reality of God and describing what happens to a human when approaching the divinity. For al-Ghazālī there is no better similitude for explaining the oneness of God's being and how that relates to creation than the characteristics of light. Hence, *The Niche* elucidates the meaning of *tawḥīd* through commenting on the Qurʾānic assertion that God is light.

Summary of the text

The monograph is three chapters long, and the critical Arabic edition (1964) upon which this translation is based runs to sixty-four pages. The first and longest chapter explains the meaning of the first sentence of the Light Verse: "God is the light of the heavens and the earth," by outlining a metaphysics of light based upon the cardinal teaching of the Qurʾān and *ḥadīth: tawḥīd,* the declaration that God is one. This metaphysical scheme is explained by presenting an ontology, epistemology, cosmology, and psychology based upon the teaching that the real light is God and that anything else called light is a metaphor. From this perspective, true light is pure existence and knowledge, and the whole of creation is seen as nothing but the manifestation of God's light. The remaining two chapters expand upon the main points mentioned in the first, and particularly on how to perceive God's light correctly.

The second chapter details the cosmology and psychology already mentioned. Al-Ghazālī explains that the goal of human existence is to traverse the unseen worlds of the universe to achieve nearness to God through an inward transformation of the soul that leads to gaining knowledge of the cosmos, oneself, and God. He describes the interrelated hierarchical natures of the human reality and the universe, and discusses how inner purification of the soul brings about the journeying to God.

An important concept he employs is that all things in the visible world are similitudes *(mithāl)* of things that exist in the unseen worlds that stand above it in the hierarchical cosmos. There is a qualitative correspondence between all things that exist in these numerous worlds. Put another way, the qualities of all things in the visible world provide knowledge of things in the unseen world and vice versa.[58] By ascending to the unseen world, one can obtain knowledge of things in the visible world; and by meditating on the qualities of things in the visible world, one can gain knowledge of things in the unseen world. The Qurʾān contains similitudes that, when interpreted in this manner, provide knowledge of the visible and unseen aspects of both the universe and the human being. The unseen aspect of a human being is called the "soul," which in traditional Islamic psychology is the source of life, self-awareness (including our faculties of perception), knowledge, and emotions.

Al-Ghazālī says that the five similitudes mentioned in the Light Verse can be understood to stand for the five perceptual faculties of the human soul. In this case the lamp, the niche, the glass, the tree, and the olive of the Light Verse are all visible, existent things whose characteristics point to the attributes of these five faculties: senses, imagination, reflection, the rational faculty, and the prophetic faculty. In the second chapter, al-Ghazālī interprets these Qurʾānic similitudes in such a way as to explain what happens to the soul when it journeys to God through the inward purification that is accomplished through following the teachings of Islam. The greater the soul's purification, the more one is able to perceive God's light and gain true knowledge of things in the cosmos through these five faculties. However, only the prophets and great saints have actualized the highest faculty, the "holy prophetic spirit," in which the perception of God's light is most complete.

The last chapter is an exegesis of the Veils *Ḥadīth.* Here al-Ghazālī defines the various types of people who are veiled from God's light in terms of their religious beliefs and practices. He summarizes the previous discussions of God as light, and how humans perceive this light through the five faculties of the soul. He shows that the veiling of these different modes of perception has various effects on peoples' religious beliefs and behavior. Al-Ghazālī says that these veils are really the various obstacles that prevent the five faculties of human perception from comprehending the true nature of God's light, thereby causing people to be ignorant of the world around them and of God.

People are veiled by sheer darkness, darkness mixed with light, and light alone. These veils cause the five faculties of perception to function improperly. Selfish appetites *(shahwa)* and anger *(ghaḍab)* are dark veils; corrupt beliefs *(iᶜtiqādāt)* and imagination *(khayāl)* are veils of light and darkness; and corrupt rational analogies *(muqāyasāt)* are veils of light. All these veils distort perception of the source of light: God. Hence, people end up worshipping the gods of their deceived perceptions—idols, their own souls, a supreme being located "up," and other objects of worship mentioned in the text. For correct worship, the faculties must be cleansed of these distorting influences. Purification of this corruption comes through sincere religious practice, the goal of which is to actualize the highest faculty, the holy prophetic spirit, which is found fully in the prophets and partially in the great saints. However, even this faculty at some point in the journey to God becomes a limitation. The highest stage of realizing True Light is to become extinct *(fanā᾿)* from all the faculties, at which point all veils are burned away and there remains God's light alone, illuminating the hearts of the travelers, whom al-Ghazālī calls "those who have arrived" *(al-wāṣilūn)*.

> The august glories of His face burn them up, and the ruling authority of majesty overcomes them. In their essences they are effaced and annihilated. They become extinct *[fanā᾿]*[59] from themselves, so that they cease observing themselves. Nothing remains save the One, the Real. The meaning of His words, "Everything is perishing except His face" [Qur᾿ān 28:88], becomes for them a taste and a state. (p. 52)

After extinction from themselves is achieved, the faculties of the soul return but are now transformed by the shining of God's light within the heart. The Light Verse employs the five similitudes to express the nature of the five faculties of the soul of a person whose inner reality is now the locus of divine illumination, free from the distorting veils of ignorance.

Conclusion

In *The Niche of Lights,* al-Ghazālī expresses a worldview—a way of giving meaning to reality through presenting an interrelated cosmology and psychology—by which a thoughtful Muslim might explain what the universe is and what it means to be human in a manner that is in harmony with the Qur'ān and *ḥadīth.* The underlying principle that guides the text is *tawḥīd,* thus placing it in the mainstream of Islamic thought.

Al-Ghazālī's later writings present an attempt to unify in unpretentious rhetoric Islamic law, theology, philosophy, and inner piety as diverse expressions of the central Islamic message of *tawḥīd.* If *tawḥīd* implies a "making one, or uniting" then al-Ghazālī attempted in his life and work to unite the diverse strands of Islamic thought and practice under the rubric of the message of the Qur'ān and *ḥadīth.* Works like the *Revivification* attempted to do this on a grand scale while speaking to the learned members of the community. *The Niche of Lights* is a much smaller, more readable, and more concise work which brings out the essence of Islamic teachings in a way that is intellectually meaningful and existentially satisfying. As a text, it provides an answer to why "God is the light of the heavens and the earth," and at the same time it shows that in order to really understand this, one must undertake a journey whose goal is to perceive this as clearly as one perceives the sun.

A note on the translation

The Niche of Lights has previously been translated into French by Roger Deladrière, into German by ʿAbd-Elsamad ʿAbd-Elhamīd Elschazlī, into Italian by Laura Veccia Vaglieri and Roberto Rubinacci, and into English by W. H. T. Gairdner.[60] The French and German editions are quite recent, while the English translation was published in 1924.

The Arabic edition upon which this translation is based is the critical edition published in Cairo in 1964, edited and introduced by Abū al-ʿAlā ʿAfīfī. The Arabic text of this book is taken from ʿAfīfī's edition, with minor changes.

I checked my own translation against that of both Deladrière and Gairdner. Deladrière's translation is more literal than Gairdner's. I found that Gairdner divides the text where al-Ghazālī does not, and he is not consistent in his use of technical terms. Deladrière is more careful and consistent with his terminology and follows the Arabic text closely. Deladrière and I used the same critical Arabic version of *The Niche of Lights.* In my own translation, I have attempted to be as literal as possible and to remain consistent in the use of technical terms.

بسم الله الرحمن الرحيم

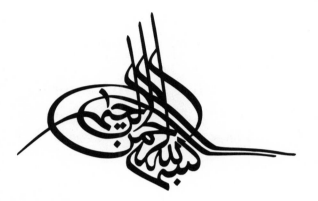

In the name of God, the Compassionate, the Merciful

[Author's Introduction]

My Lord, Thou hast blessed, so increase by Thy bounty!

(1) Praise belongs to God, Effuser of Lights, Opener of Eyes, Unveiler of Mysteries, Lifter of Coverings. And blessings be upon Muḥammad, light of lights, master of the devotees, beloved of the All-Compeller, bringer of good news from the All-Forgiver, warner on behalf of the Overwhelming, tamer of the unbelievers, disgracer of the wicked. And blessings be upon his family and companions—the good, the pure, the chosen.

(2) Now to begin: You asked me, O noble brother—may God lead you to search for the greatest felicity, train you to ascend to the highest summit, anoint your insight with the light of Reality, and cleanse all other than the Real from your inmost center—that I unfold for you the mysteries of the divine lights, along with an interpretation of the apparent meanings of those recited verses and narrated reports that allude to the divine lights, like His words, "God is the light of the heavens and the earth" [24:35]; and [that I explain] the sense of His comparing this with the niche, the glass, the lamp, the olive, and the tree; and likewise the saying of the Prophet: "God has seventy veils of light and darkness; were He to lift them, the august glories of His face would burn up everyone whose eyesight perceived Him."[1]

(3) With your question you have climbed a difficult slope, one before whose upper regions the eyes of the observers fall back. You have knocked at a locked door that is not to be opened except for the firmly rooted possessors of knowledge. What is more, not every mystery is to

بسم الله الرحمن الرحيم

رب أنعمت فزدْ بفضلك

(١) الحمد لله فائض الأنوار وفاتح الأبصار، وكاشف الأسرار ورافع الأستار. والصلاة على محمد نور الأنوار وسيد الأبرار وحبيب الجبار وبشير الغفّار ونذير القهار، وقامع الكفار وفاضح الفجّار؛ وعلى آله وأصحابه الطيبين الطاهرين الأخيار.

(٢) أما بعد فقد سألتنى أيها الأخ الكريم قيّضك الله لطلب السعادة الكبرى، ورشحك للعروج إلى الذروة العليا، وكحّل بنور الحقيقة بصيرتك، ونقّى عمّا سوى الحق سريرتك، أن أبث إليك أسرار الأنوار الإلهية مقرونة بتأويل ما يشير إليه ظواهر الآيات المتلوة والأخبار المروية مثل قوله تعالى «الله نور السموات والأرض» ومعنى تمثيله ذلك بالمشكاة والزجاجة والمصباح والزيت والشجرة، مع قوله عليه السلام «إن لله سبعين حجاباً من نور وظلمة وإنه لو كشفها لأحرقت سبحاتُ وجهِهِ كلَ من أدركه بصره».

(٣) ولقد ارتقيت بسؤالك مرتقىً صعباً تنخفض دون أعاليه أعين الناظرين؛ وقرعْت باباً مغلقاً لا يُفتَح إلا للعلماء الراسخين. ثم ليس كل سر

be unveiled and divulged, and not every reality is to be presented and disclosed. Indeed, "the breasts of the free are the graves of the mysteries."[2] One of the gnostics has said, "To divulge the mystery of Lordship is unbelief."[3] Indeed, the Master of the First and the Last [the Prophet] said, "There is a kind of knowledge like the guise of the hidden; none knows it except the knowers of God. When they speak of it, none denies it except those who are arrogantly deluded about God."[4] And when the people of arrogant delusion become many, it becomes necessary to preserve the coverings upon the face of the mysteries. But I see you as one whose breast has been opened up[5] by God through light and whose innermost consciousness has been kept free of the darknesses of delusion. Hence, in this discipline I will not be niggardly toward you in alluding to sparks and flashes or giving symbols of realities and subtleties, for the fear in holding back knowledge from those worthy of it is not less than that in disseminating it to those not worthy of it.

He who bestows knowledge on the ignorant wastes it,
And he who withholds it from the worthy has done them wrong.[6]

(4) So be satisfied with abridged allusions and brief hints, since the verification of this discussion would call for laying down principles and explaining details which my present moment does not allow, nor do my concern and thought turn toward such things. The keys of hearts are in God's hand; He opens hearts when He wills, as He wills, and how He wills. The only thing opening up at this moment is three chapters.

يُكشَف ويُفشى، ولا كل حقيقة تعرض وتُجلَى؛ بل صدور الأحرار قبور الأسرار. ولقد قال بعض العارفين «إفشاء سر الربوبية كفر». بل قال سيد الأولين والآخرين صلى الله عليه «إن من العلم كهيئة المكنون لا يعلمه إلا العلماء بالله، فإذا نطقوا به لم ينكره إلا أهل الغِرّة بالله،» ومهما كثر أهل الاغترار وجب حفظ الأستار على وجه الأسرار. لكنى أراك مشروح الصدر بالله بالنور، منزه السر عن ظلمات الغرور فلا أشح عليك في هذا الفن بالإشارة إلى لوامع ولوائح؛ والرمز إلى حقائق ودقائق. فليس الخوف في كف العلم عن أهله بأقل منه في بثه إلى غير أهله.

فمن مَنَحَ الجّهال علماً أضاعه ومن مَنَع المستوجبين فقد ظلم

(٤) فاقنع بإشارات مختصرة وتلويحات موجزة؛ فإن تحقيق القول فيه يستدعى تمهيد أصول وشرح فصول ليس يتسع الآن لها وقتى، وليس ينصرف أليه همى وفكرتى. ومفاتيح القلوب بيد الله يفتحها إذا شاء كما شاء بما يشاء. وإنما الذى ينفتح في الوقت فصول ثلاثة.

The First Chapter

Clarifying that the real light is God
and that the name "light" for everything else
is sheer metaphor, without reality

(1) This is clarified through coming to know the meaning of the word "light" in the first sense of the term, following the view of the common people; then in the second sense, following the view of the elect; then in the third sense, following the view of the elect of the elect. You will then come to know the degrees and realities of the mentioned lights that are ascribed to the elect of the elect. It will be unveiled to you, when the degrees of these lights become manifest, that God is the highest and furthest light, and, when their realities become unveiled, that He is the real, true light—He alone, without any partner in that.

(2) Regarding the first sense of the word, for the common people, "light" alludes to manifestation. Manifestation is a relative affair, since without doubt a thing may be manifest to one person while remaining nonmanifest to another; hence, a thing is relatively manifest and relatively nonmanifest. Its manifestation is unquestionably ascribed to the faculties of perception. The strongest and most obvious of these, in the view of the common people, are the senses, among which is the sense of sight.

(3) In relation to visual sensation, things are of three kinds: First are those which cannot be seen in themselves, such as dark bodies. Second are those which can be seen in themselves but by which other things cannot be seen, such as bright bodies or stars and glowing coals that are not aflame. Third are those which can be seen in themselves and by which

الفصل الأول

في بيان أن النور الحق هو الله تعالى وأن اسم النور لغيره مجاز محض لا حقيقة له

(١) وبيانه بأن يعرف معنى النور بالوضع الأول عند العوام، ثم بالوضع الثاني عند الخواص، ثم بالوضع الثالث عند خواص الخواص. ثم تعرف درجات الأنوار المذكورة المنسوبة إلى خواص الخواص وحقائقها لينكشف لك عند ظهور درجاتها أن الله تعالى هو النور الأعلى الأقصى، وعند انكشاف حقائقها أنه النور الحق الحقيق وحده لا شريك له فيه.

(٢) أما الوضع الأول عند العامى فالنور يشير إلى الظهور، والظهور أمر إضافي: إذ يظهر الشيء لا محالة لإنسان ويبطن عن غيره: فيكون ظاهرا بالإضافة وباطناً بالإضافة. وإضافة ظهوره إلى الإدراكات لا محالة. وأقوى الإدراكات وأجلاها عند العوام الحواسّ، ومنها حاسة البصر.

(٣) والأشياء بالإضافة إلى الحس البصرى ثلاثة أقسام: منها ما لا يبصر بنفسه كالأجسام المظلمة. ومنها ما يبصَر بنفسه ولا يبصَر به غيره كالأجسام المضيئة كالكواكب وجمرة النار إذا لم تكن مشتعلة. ومنها ما يبصَر بنفسه

other things can be seen, such as the sun, the moon, a lamp, and a flaming fire. "Light" is a name that belongs to this third kind.

(4) Sometimes the name "light" is applied to that which flows forth from these bodies onto the manifest dimensions of dense bodies. Then it is said, "The earth is illuminated," "The light of the sun has fallen on the earth," and "The light of the lamp has fallen on the wall and the clothing." Sometimes the name "light" is applied to these same radiant bodies, since they are also lit up in themselves.

(5) In sum, "light" consists of that which is seen in itself and through which other things are seen, such as the sun. This is its definition and reality in the first sense.

A fine point

(6) The mystery and spirit of light is manifestation to perception. Perception is conditional upon the existence of light and also upon the existence of the seeing eye. For light is that which is manifest and makes manifest; but for the blind, lights are neither manifest nor do they make things manifest. Hence, the seeing spirit and the existence of manifest light are equivalent in that they are inescapable supports for perception. What is more, the seeing spirit is superior to the manifest light, since it perceives and through it perception takes place. As for light, it neither perceives nor does perception take place through it; rather, when it is there, perception takes place. Therefore, it is more appropriate that the name "light" be given to the seeing light than to the seen light.

(7) People apply the name "light" to the light of the seeing eye. They say that the light of the bat's eyesight is weak, the light of the nearsighted man's eyesight is weak, the blind man lacks the light of eyesight, and the color black gathers and strengthens the light of eyesight. [They say that] the divine wisdom singled out the color black

ويبصَر به أيضاً غيره كالشمس والقمر والسراج والنير ان المشتعلة. والنور اسم لهذا القسم الثالث.

(٤) ثم تارة يطلق على ما يفيض من الأجسام على ظواهر الأجسام الكثيفة، فيقال استنارت الأرض ووقع نور الشمس على الأرض ونور السراج على الحائط والثوب. وتارة يطلق على نفس هذه الأجسام المشرقة لأنها أيضاً في نفسها مستنيرة.

(٥) وعلى الجملة فالنور عبارة عما يبصَر بنفسه ويبصَر به غيره كالشمس. هذا حده وحقيقته بالوضع الأول.

دقيقة

(٦) لما كان سر النور وروحه هو الظهور للإدراك، وكان الإدراك موقوفاً على وجود النور وعلى وجود العين الباصرة أيضاً: إذ النور هو الظاهر المظهِر؛ وليس شيء من الأنوار ظاهراً في حق العميان ولا مظهراً. فقد تساوى الروح الباصرة والنور الظاهر في كونه ركناً لا بد منه للإدراك ثم ترجّح عليه في أن الروح الباصرة هي المدركة وبها الإدراك. وأما النور فليس بمدرك ولا به الإدراك، بل عنده الإدراك. فكان اسم النور بالنور الباصر أحق منه بالنور المبصَر.

(٧) وأطلقوا اسم النور على نور العين المبصرة فقالوا في الخفّاش إن نور عينه ضعيف، وفي الأعمش إنه ضعف نور بصره، وفي الأعمى إنه فقد نور البصر، وفي السواد إنه يجمع نور البصر ويقويه، وإن الأجفان إنما خصتها الحكمة

for the eyelids and made them surround the eye in order to gather the brightness of the eye. As for the color white, it disperses the eye's brightness and weakens its light to such a degree that persistent looking at radiant whiteness, or at the light of the sun, dazzles and effaces the light of the eye, just as the weak becomes effaced next to the strong.[1]

(8) Thus, you have come to know that the seeing spirit is called light, and why it is called light, and why this name is to be preferred. This is the second sense of the term, the sense followed by the elect.

A fine point

(9) Know that eyesight's light is branded with many kinds of imperfection: It sees other things while not seeing itself. It does not see what is far away from it. It does not see what is behind a veil. It sees manifest things, but not nonmanifest ones. It sees some of the existent things, but not all of them. It sees the finite things, but not that which is infinite. And it commits many errors in seeing: It sees the large as small, the far as near, the motionless as moving, and the moving as motionless. These seven imperfections are never separate from the outward eye. If there is an eye to be found among the eyes, free of all these imperfections, tell me whether or not it is more worthy of the name "light"!

(10) Know also that the heart of the human being has an eye whose qualities of perfection are precisely this [lack of the seven imperfections]. It is this eye that is sometimes called the rational faculty, sometimes the spirit, and sometimes the human soul. However, put aside these expressions; because when they become many, they make the person of weak insight imagine many meanings. What we mean by this eye is that meaning whereby the rational person is distinguished from suckling infants, animals, and madmen. Therefore, let us call it the "rational faculty," in keeping with the technical terms of most people. Therefore, we say:

الإلهية بلون السواد وجعل العين محفوفة بها لتجمع ضوء العين. وأما البياض فيفرق ضوء العين ويضعف نوره، حتى إن إدامة النظر إلى البياض المشرق، بل إلى نور الشمس يبهر نور العين ويمحقه كما ينمحق الضعيف في جنب القوى.

(٨) فقد عرفت بهذا أن الروح الباصر سمى نوراً، وأنه لِمَ سمّى نوراً، وأنه لِمَ كان بهذا الاسم أولى. وهذا هو الوضع الثانى وهو وضع الخواص.

دقيقة

(٩) إعلم أن نور بصر العين موسوم بأنواع النقصان: فإنه يبصر غيره ولا يبصر نفسه، ولا يبصر ما بَعُد منه ولا يبصر ما هو وراء حجاب. ويبصر من الأشياء ظاهرها دون باطنها؛ ويبصر من الموجودات بعضها دون كلها. ويبصر أشياء متناهية ولا يبصر ما لا نهاية له. ويغلط كثيراً في إبصاره: فيرى الكبير صغيراً والبعيد قريباً والساكن متحركاً والمتحرك ساكناً. فهذه سبع نقائص لا تفارق العين الظاهرة. فإن كان في الأعين عين منزهة عن هذه النقائص كلها فليت شعرى هل هو أولى باسم النور أم لا؟

(١٠) واعلم أن في قلب الإنسان عيناً هذه صفة كمالها وهى التى يعبّر عنها تارة بالعقل وتارة بالروح وتارة بالنفس الإنسانى. ودعْ عنك العبارات فإنها إذا كثرت أو همَت عند ضعيف البصيرة كثرة المعانى. فنعنى به المعنى الذى يتميز به العاقل عن الطفل الرضيع وعن البهيمة وعن المجنون. ولنسمه «عقلاً» متابعة للجمهور في الاصطلاح فنقول:

(11) The rational faculty is more worthy to be named light than the outward eye, because its measure is lifted beyond the seven imperfections, which are: [First,] that the eye cannot see itself, while the rational faculty perceives other things and its own attributes. Since it perceives itself as knowing and powerful, it perceives its knowledge of itself, it perceives its knowledge of its knowledge of itself, it perceives its knowledge of its knowledge of its knowledge of itself, and so on *ad infinitum*. This is a characteristic that is inconceivable in that which perceives through bodily instruments. And behind this lies a mystery that would take too long to explain.

(12) The second imperfection is that the eye does not see what is far from it and what is extremely close to it, while near and far are equal for the rational faculty. In a glance it ascends to the highest heavens, and with a look it descends down into the confines of the earths. Indeed, when the realities have been ascertained, it will be unveiled that the rational faculty is so pure that the meanings of near and far that are assigned to bodily things cannot revolve in the regions of its holiness. The rational faculty is a sample of the light of God; and a sample does not lack a certain resemblance, though it never climbs to the peak of equality. Perhaps this discussion has moved you to fathom the mystery of the Prophet's words, "Verily, God created Adam upon His own form."[2] But to enter into this discussion now is inappropriate.

(13) The third imperfection is that the eye does not perceive what lies behind veils, while the rational faculty moves freely around the throne [of God, around His] footstool, [around] that which lies behind the veils of the heavens, and around the higher plenum and the most exalted dominion [of God]. In the same way, it moves freely around its own specific world and nearby kingdom—that is, its own body. Or rather, no realities whatsoever are veiled from the rational faculty. As for the veiling undergone by the rational faculty when it does become veiled, this is the rational faculty's veiling itself by itself due to certain attributes that are associated with it. In a similar way, the eye becomes veiled from itself when the eyelids are closed. You will come to know about this in chapter three of this book.

(14) The fourth imperfection is that the eye perceives the manifest dimension and surface of things, not their nonmanifest dimension. Or rather, [it perceives] their frames and forms, not their realities. But the rational faculty penetrates nonmanifest dimensions and mysteries of

(١١) العقل أولى بأن يسمى نوراً من العين الظاهرة لرفعة قدره عن النقائص السبع وهو أن العين لا تبصر نفسها، والعقل يدرك غيره ويدرك صفات نفسه: إذ يدرك نفسه عالماً وقادراً: ويدرك علم نفسه ويدرك علمه بعلم نفسه وعلمه بعلمه بعلم نفسه إلى غير نهاية. وهذه خاصيةٌ لا تتصور لما يدرك بآلة الأجسام. ووراءه سر يطول شرحه.

(١٢) والثانى أن العين لا تبصر مابَعُد منها ولا ما قرب منها قرباً مفرطاً: والعقل يستوى عنده القريب والبعيد: يعرج في تطريفة إلى أعلى السموات رقياً، وينزل في لحظة إلى تخوم الأرضين هوِياً. بل إذا حقت الحقائق انكشف أنه منزه عن أن تحوم بجنبات قدسه معانى القرب والبعد الذى يفرض بين الأجسام، فإنه أنموذج من نور الله تعالى، ولا يخلو الأنموذج عن محاكاة، وإن كان لا يرقي إلى ذروة المساواة. وهذا ربما هزّك للتفطن لسر قوله عليه السلام «إن الله خلق آدم على صورته» فلست أرى الخوض فيه الآن.

(١٣) الثالث أن العين لا تدرك ما وراء الحجب، والعقل يتصرف في العرش والكرسى وما وراء حجب السموات، وفي الملأ الأعلى والملكوت الأسمى كتصرفه في عالمه الخاص ومملكته القريبة أعنى بدنه الخاص. بل الحقائق كلها لا تحتجب عن العقل. وأما حجاب العقل حيث يحجب فمن نفسه لنفسه بسبب صفات هى مقارنة له تضاهى حجاب العين من نفسه عند تغميض الأجفان. وستعرف هذا في الفصل الثالث من الكتاب.

(١٤) الرابع أن العين تدرك من الأشياء ظاهرها وسطحها الأعلى دون باطنها؛ بل قوالبها وصورها دون حَقائقها. والعقل يتغلغل إلى بواطن الأشياء

things, perceiving their realities and their spirits. It searches out their secondary cause, their deeper cause, their ultimate end, and the wisdom [in their existence]. [It discovers] what a thing was created from, how it was created, why it was created, and how many meanings were involved in its being brought together and compounded. [It finds out] on what level of existence a thing has come to dwell, what its relationship is with its Creator, and what its relationship is with the rest of His creatures. It makes many more discoveries which to explain would take too long, so we will cut this short.

(15) The fifth imperfection is that the eye sees only some existent things, since it fails to see the objects of the rational faculty and [also] many of the objects of sensation. It does not perceive sounds, odors, flavors, heat, cold, and the perceptual faculties—namely, the faculties of hearing, seeing, smelling, and tasting. Nor, moreover, [does it perceive] the inner attributes of the soul, such as joy, happiness, grief, sadness, pain, pleasure, passionate love, appetite, power, desire, knowledge, and so forth. These existent things cannot be enumerated or counted. Hence, the eye has a narrow domain and an abridged channel. It cannot pass beyond the world of colors and shapes, which are the most base of existent things. After all, bodies, at root, are the most base kinds of existent things, and colors and shapes are some of their most base accidents.

(16) All existent things are the domain of the rational faculty, since it perceives those things which we have listed and an even greater number which we have not. Hence, the rational faculty moves freely over all things and passes an indisputable and truthful judgment upon them. Inward mysteries are apparent to it, and hidden meanings are disclosed to it. How can the outward eye vie with it and seek to keep up with it in worthiness for the name "light"?

(17) No, the eye is light in relation to other things, but it is darkness in relation to the rational faculty. Or rather, the eye is one of the rational faculty's spies. It has been entrusted with the most base of the rational faculty's storehouses—the storehouse of the world of colors and shapes—in order that the eye may take news of this world up to the rational faculty's presence. Thereupon, the rational faculty decides about these reports in virtue of what its piercing view and penetrating judgment demand. The five senses are the rational faculty's spies, and besides these it has spies in the nonmanifest dimension: imagination, fancy, reflection,

وأسرارها ويدرك حقائقها وأرواحها، ويستنبط سببها وعلتها وغايتها وحكمتها، وأنها ممّ خلق وكيف خلق، ولِمَ خلق، ومِن كم معنى جمع وركّب، وعلى أى مرتبة في الوجود نزل، وما نسبته إلى خالقها وما نسبتها إلى سائر مخلوقاته، إلى مباحث أُخر يطول شرحها نرى الإيجاز فيها أولى.

(١٥) الخامس أن العين تبصر بعض الموجودات أذ تقصر عن جميع المعقولات وعن كثير من المحسوسات: إذ لا تدرك الأصوات والروائح والطعوم والحرارة والبرودة والقوى المدركة: أعنى قوة السمع والبصر والشم والذوق، بل الصفات الباطنة النفسانية كالفرح والسرور والغم والحزن والألم واللذة والعشق والشهوة والقدرة والإرادة والعلم إلى غير ذلك من موجودات لا تحصى ولا تعد؛ فهو ضيق المجال مختصر المجرى لا تسعه مجاوزة الألوان والأشكال وهما أخس الموجودات: فإن الأجسام في أصلها أخس أقسام الموجودات، والألوان والأشكال من أخس أعراضها.

(١٦) فالموجودات كلها مجال العقل؛ إذ يدرك هذه الموجودات التى عددناها وما لم نعددها، وهو الأكثر: فيتصرف في جميعها ويحكم عليها حكماً يقينياً صادقاً. فالأسرار الباطنة عنده ظاهرة، والمعانى الخفية عنده جلية. فمن أين للعين الظاهرة مساماته ومجاراته في استحقاق اسم النور؟

(١٧) كلا إنها نور بالإضافة إلى غيرها؛ لكنها ظلمة بالإضافة إليه. بل هى جاسوس من جواسيسه؛ وكله بأخس خزائنه وهى خزانة الألوان والأشكال لترفع إلى حضرته أخبارها فيقضى فيها بما يقتضيه رأيه الثاقب وحكمه النافذ. والحواس الخمس جواسيسه. وله في الباطن جواسيس سواها من خيال ووهم

recollection, and memory. Beyond these spies are servants and soldiers who are subject to the rational faculty in its own world. The rational faculty subjugates them and has free disposal over them just as a king subjugates his vassals, or even more intensely. To explain this would take too long, and I have mentioned this in one of the books of the *Iḥyāʾ*, "*ʿAjāʾib al-qalb*" [The wonders of the heart].[3]

(18) The sixth imperfection is that the eye does not see what is infinite, since it sees the attributes of bodies, and bodies can only be conceived of as finite. But the rational faculty perceives objects of knowledge, and it is inconceivable that objects of knowledge be finite. Certainly, when the rational faculty observes differentiated knowledge, then what is actually present with it can only be finite. But it has the potential to perceive what is infinite. However, to explain this would take too long. If you desire an example of this, take it from things that are obvious: The rational faculty perceives numbers, and numbers are infinite. Or rather, it perceives the multiples of the numbers two, three, and so on, and no one can conceive of an end to these. It perceives the different types of relationships that exist among numbers, and an end to these is also inconceivable. Finally, it perceives its own knowledge of something, the knowledge of its knowledge of that thing, and its knowledge of its knowledge of its knowledge. Hence, in this single instance the rational faculty's potential is infinite.

(19) The seventh imperfection is that the eye sees large things as small. Hence, it sees the sun as having the size of a shield and the stars in the form of dinars scattered upon a blue carpet. The rational faculty, however, perceives the stars and the sun as many times larger than the earth. The eye sees the stars as though they were motionless, [sees] shadows as motionless in front of it, and [sees] a boy as motionless during his growth. But the rational faculty perceives that the boy is in motion through his perpetual growth and increase, that the shadow is perpetually moving, and that the stars move many miles at each instant. Thus the Prophet said to Gabriel, "Does the sun move?" He answered, "No—Yes!" The Prophet then said, "How is that?" Gabriel replied, "From the time I said 'No' to the time I said 'Yes,' it moved a journey of five hundred years."[4]

وفكر وذكر وحفظ؛ ووراءهم خدم وجنود مسخرة له في عالمه الخاص يستسخرهم ويتصرف فيهم استسخار الملك عبيده بل أشد. وشرح ذلك يطول. وقد ذكرناه في كتاب «عجائب القلب» من كتب الإحياء.

(١٨) السادس أن العين لا تبصر ما لا نهاية له، فإنها تبصر صفات الأجسام والأجسام لا تتصور إلا متناهية. والعقل يدرك المعلومات؛ والمعلومات لا يتصور أن تكون متناهية. نعم إذا لاحظ العلوم المفصلة فلا يكون الحاضر الحاصل عنده إلا متناهياً. لكن في قوته إدراك ما لا نهاية له. وشرح ذلك يطول. فإن أردت له مثالاً فخذه من الجليات، فإنه يدرك الأعداد ولا نهاية لها؛ بل يدرك تضعيفات الاثنين والثلاثة وسائر الأعداد ولا يتصور لها نهاية. ويدرك أنواعاً من النسب بين الأعداد لا يتصور التناهى عليها: بل يدرك علمه بالشيء وعلمه بعلمه بالشيء، وعلمه بعلمه بعلمه. فقوته في هذا الواحد لا تقف عند نهاية.

(١٩) السابع أن العين تبصر الكبير صغيراً، فترى الشمس في مقدار مِجَنّ والكواكب في صور دنانير منثورة على بساط أزرق. والعقل يدرك أن الكواكب والشمس أكبر من الأرض أضعافاً مضاعفة؛ والعين ترى الكواكب ساكنة، بل ترى الظل بين يديه ساكناً، وترى الصبي ساكناً في مقداره، والعقل يدرك أن الصبي متحرك في النشوء والتزايد على الدوام، والظل متحرك دائماً، والكواكب تتحرك في كل لحظة أميالاً كثيرة كما قال صلى الله عليه لجبريل عليه السلام: «أزالت الشمس»؟ فقال «لا نعم!» قال كيف؟ قال «منذ قلت، لا إلى أن قلت، نعم، قد تحرك مسيرة خمسمائة سنة».

(20) Eyesight commits many sorts of errors, while the rational faculty is free of them. You may say, "We see the people of the rational faculty committing errors in their consideration." But you should know that these people have imaginings, fancies, and beliefs and that they suppose that the properties of these are the same as those of the rational faculty. Hence, the errors are attributable to these things. We explained all this in the books *Miʿyār al-ʿilm* [The standard of knowledge] and *Miḥakk al-naẓar* [The touchstone of consideration].

(21) As for the rational faculty, once it disengages itself from the coverings of fancy and imagination, it is inconceivable that it can commit an error. On the contrary, it will see things as they are in themselves. However, for the rational faculty to achieve disengagement is extremely difficult. Its disengagement from the pull of these things only becomes perfected after death, when the wrappings are lifted, the mysteries are disclosed, and everyone meets face to face the good or evil that he has sent forward.[5] He witnesses a book that "leaves nothing behind, great or small, but it has numbered it" [18:49]. At that time it is said, "Therefore, We have removed from thee thy covering, so thine eyesight today is piercing" [50:22]. This covering is the covering of imagination, fancy, and other things. At this time those deluded by their fancies, their corrupt beliefs, and their unreal imaginations say, "Our Lord, we have seen and heard; now return us, that we may do good works, for we have sure faith" [32:12].

(22) You have come to know through this discussion that the eye is more worthy of the name "light" than the well-known light. Further, you have come to know that the rational faculty is more worthy of the name "light" than the eye. Indeed, there is such a difference between the two that it is correct to say that the rational faculty is more worthy—or, rather, that the rational faculty in truth deserves the name alone.

A fine point

(23) Know that although rational faculties see, the objects that they see are not with them in the same manner. On the contrary, some of [the objects] are with them as if they were actually present, such as self-evident knowledge. For example, the rational faculty knows that a single thing cannot be both eternal and created, or both existent and nonexistent;

(٢٠) وأنواع غلط البصر كثيرة، والعقل منزه عنها. فإن قلت: نرى العقلاء يغلطون في نظرهم فاعلم أن فيهم خيالات وأوهاماً واعتقادات يظنون أحكامها أحكام العقل؛ فالغلط منسوب إليها. وقد شرحنا مجامعها في كتاب «معيار العلم» وكتاب «محك النظر».

(٢١) فأما العقل إذا تجرد عن غشاوة الوهم والخيال لم يتصور أن يغلط؛ بل رأى الأشياء على ما هى عليه، وفي تجريده عسر عظيم. وإنما يكمل تجرده عن هذه النوازع بعد الموت، وعند ذلك ينكشف الغطاء وتنجلى الأسرار ويصادف كل أحد ما قدّم من خير أو شر مُحضَراً؛ ويشاهد كتاباً «لا يغادر صغيرة ولا كبيرة إلا أحصاها»، وعنده يقال «فكشفنا عنك غطاءك فبصرك اليوم حديد». وإنما الغطاء غطاء الخيال والوهم وغيرهما؛ وعنده يقول المغرور بأوهامه واعتقاداته الفاسدة وخيالاته الباطلة «ربنا أبصَرنا وسمعنا فارجعنا نعمل صالحاً» الآية.

(٢٢) فقد عرفت بهذا أن العين أولى باسم النور من النور المعروف، ثم عرفت أن العقل أولى باسم النور من العين. بل بينهما من التفاوت ما يصح معه أن يقال إنه أولى بل الحق أنه المستحق للاسم دونه.

دقيقة

(٢٣) اعلم أن العقول وإن كانت مبصرة، فليست المبصرات كلها عندها على وتيرة واحدة، بل بعضها يكون عندها كأنه حاضر كالعلوم الضرورية مثل علمه بأن الشيء الواحد لا يكون قديماً حادثاً ولا يكون موجوداً معدوماً،

that a single statement cannot be both true and false; that when a judgment about a thing has been made, the same judgment can be made for similar things; and that when a more specific thing exists, the more general must exist. Thus, if blackness exists, color must exist; and if man exists, animals must exist. But the rational faculty does not see the contrary of this as necessary, since the existence of blackness does not necessarily follow from the existence of color, nor the existence of man from the existence of animals. There are also other self-evident statements pertaining to necessary, possible, and impossible things.

(24) There are other objects of sight which, when submitted to the rational faculty, do not always join with it. Or rather, it must be shaken, and fire must be kindled within it; it must take notice of them by having them called to its attention. This is the case with affairs that pertain to rational consideration. However, nothing other than the speech of wisdom can bring things to its attention; for when the light of wisdom radiates, the rational faculty comes to see in actuality, after having been able to see only potentially.

(25) The greatest wisdom is the speech of God. Among [those things that] He has spoken is the Qurʾān specifically. For the eye of the rational faculty, the Qurʾān's verses take the place that is occupied by the sun's light for the outward eye, since seeing occurs through it. Hence, it is appropriate for the Qurʾān to be named "light," just as the light of the sun is named "light." The Qurʾān is like the light of the sun, while the rational faculty is like the light of the eye. In this way, we should understand the meaning of His words, "Therefore, have faith in God and His messenger and in the light which We have sent down" [64:8] and His words, "A proof has now come to you from your Lord. We have sent it down to you as a clear light" [4:174].

A supplement to this fine point

(26) You have learned from this discussion that the eye is two eyes: outward and inward. The outward eye derives from the world of sensation and visibility, while the inward eye derives from another world—namely, the world of dominion.[6] Each of these two eyes has

والقول الواحد لا يكون صدقاً وكذباً، وأن الحكم إذا ثبت للشيء جوازه ثبت لمثله، وأن الأخص إذا كان موجوداً كان الأعم واجب الوجود: فإذا وجد السواد فقد وجد اللون، وإذا وجد الإنسان فقد وجد الحيوان. وأما عكسه فلا يلزم في العقل، إذ لا يلزم من وجود اللون وجود السواد ولا من وجود الحيوان وجود الإنسان إلى غير ذلك من القضايا الضرورية في الواجبات والجائزات والمستحيلات.

(٢٤) ومنها ما لا يقارن العقلَ في كل حال إذا عرض عليه بل يحتاج إلى أن يهز أعطافه ويستورى زناده وينبه عليه بالتنبيه كالنظريات. وإنما ينبهه كلام الحكمة، فعند إشراق نور الحكمة يصير العقل مبصراً بالفعل بعد أن كان مبصراً بالقوة.

(٢٥) وأعظم الحكمة كلام الله تعالى. ومن جملة كلامه القرآن خاصة، فتكون منزلة آيات القرآن عند عين العقل منزلة نور الشمس عند العين الظاهرة إذ به يتم الإبصار. فبالحرِىّ أن يسمى القرآن نوراً كما يسمى نور الشمس نوراً فمثال القرآن نور الشمس ومثال العقل نور العين. وبهذا نفهم معنى قوله: «فآمنوا بالله ورسوله والنور الذى أنزلنا»، وقوله: «قد جاءكم برهان من ربكم وأنزلنا إليكم نوراً مبيناً»

تكملة هذه الدقيقة

(٢٦) فقد فهمت من هذا أن العين عينان: ظاهرة وباطنة: فالظاهرة من عالم الحس والشهادة، والباطنة من عالم آخر وهو عالم الملكوت. ولكل عين من

a sun and a light through which sight in these worlds is perfected. One of the two suns is outward, while the other is inward. The outward sun belongs to the visible world; it is the sun perceived by the senses. The other belongs to the world of dominion; it is the Qurʾān and the revealed books of God.

(27) When this has been unveiled to you with a complete unveiling, then the first door of the world of dominion will have been opened to you. In this world there are wonders in relation to which the visible world will be disdained. If a person does not travel to this world, then, while incapacity makes him sit in the lowlands of the visible world, he remains a beast deprived of the specific characteristic of humanity. Or rather, he is more astray than a beast, since the beast does not have the good fortune [of being able] to ascend with the wings of flight to this world [of dominion]. That is why God says, "They are like cattle—nay, rather, they are further astray" [7:179].

(28) Know also that the visible world in relation to the world of dominion is like the shell in relation to the kernel, the form and mold in relation to the spirit, darkness in relation to light, and the low in relation to the high. That is why the world of dominion is called the "high world," the "spiritual world," and the "luminous world," while standing opposite to it is the low, the corporeal, and the dark world. And do not suppose that by the "high world" we mean the heavens, since they are "high" and "above" only in respect to the visible and sensible world, and the beasts share in perceiving them.

(29) As for the servant, the door to the world of dominion will not open for him and he will not become "dominional" unless, in relation to him, the earth changes to other than the earth, and the heavens [to other than the heavens].[7] Then everything that enters into the senses and imagination will become his earth, and this includes the heavens; and whatever stands beyond the senses will be his heaven. This is the first ascent for every traveler who has begun his journey to the proximity of the Lordly Presence.

العينين شمس ونور عنده تصير كاملة الإبصار إحداهما ظاهرة والأخرى باطنة؛ والظاهرة من عالم الشهادة وهى الشمس المحسوسة، والباطنة من عالم الملكوت وهو القرآن وكتب الله تعالى المنزلة.

(٢٧) ومهما انكشف لك هذا انكشافاً تاماً فقد انفتح لك أول باب من أبواب الملكوت. وفي هذا العالم عجائب يستحقر بالإضافة إليها عالم الشهادة. وإن من لم يسافر إلى هذا العالم، وقعد به القصور في حضيض عالم الشهادة فهو بهيمة بعدُ، محروم عن خاصية الإنسانية؛ بل أضل من البهيمة إذ لم تسعد البهيمة بأجنحة الطيران إلى هذا العالم. ولذلك قال الله تعالى: «أولئك كالأنعام بل هم أضل».

(٢٨) واعلم أن الشهادة بالإضافة إلى عالم الملكوت كالقشر بالإضافة إلى اللب، وكالصورة والقالب بالإضافة إلى الروح، وكالظلمة بالإضافة إلى النور، وكالسّفل بالإضافة إلى العلو. ولذلك يسمى عالم الملكوت العالم العلوى والعالم الروحانى والعالم النورانى. وفي مقابلته السفلى والجسمانى والظلمانى. ولا تظن أنّا نعنى بالعالم العلوى السموات فإنها علو وفوق في حق عالم الشهادة والحس، ويشارك في إدراكها البهائم.

(٢٩) وأما العبد فلا يفتح له باب الملكوت ولا يصير ملكوتياً إلا ويبدل في حقه الأرض غير الأرض والسموات فيصير كل داخل تحت الحس والخيال أرضه ومن جملته السموات، وكل ما ارتفع عن الحس فسماؤه. وهذا هو المعراج الأول لكل سالك ابتدأ سفره إلى قرب الحضرة الربوبية.

(30) The human being has been reduced to the lowest of the low.[8] From there he climbs to the highest world. As for the angels, they are part of the world of dominion; they devote themselves to the Presence of the Holy, and from there they oversee the lowest world. It is for this reason that the Prophet said, "Verily, God created the creatures in darkness, and then He poured upon them some of His light."[9] He also said, "God has angels who are better informed of people's deeds than people themselves."[10]

(31) When the ascent of the prophets reaches its farthest point, when they look down from there upon the low, and when they gaze from top to bottom, they become informed of the hearts of the servants and gaze upon a certain amount of the sciences of the unseen. For when someone is in the world of dominion, he is with God, "and with Him are the keys to the unseen" [6:59]. In other words, from God the secondary causes of existent things descend into the visible world, while the visible world is one of the effects of the world of dominion. The visible world comes forth from the world of dominion just as the shadow comes forth from the thing that throws it, the fruit comes forth from the tree, and the effect comes forth from the secondary cause. The keys to knowledge of effects are found only in their secondary causes. Hence, the visible world is a similitude of the world of dominion—as will be mentioned in the clarification of the niche, the lamp, and the tree. This is because the effect cannot fail to parallel its secondary cause or to have some kind of resemblance with it, whether near or far. But this needs deep investigation. He who gains knowledge of the innermost reality of this discussion will easily have unveiled for himself the realities of the similitudes of the Qurʾān.

A fine point that goes back to the reality of light

(32) We say: That which sees itself and others is more worthy of the name "light." So if it be something that also allows other things to see, while seeing itself and others, then it is [even] more worthy of the name

(٣٠) فالإنسان مردود إلى أسفل السافلين، ومنه يترقى إلى العالم الأعلى. وأما الملائكة فإنهم جملة عالم الملكوت عاكفون في حضرة القدوس، ومنها يشرفون إلى العالم الأسفل: ولذلك قال عليه السلام «إن الله خلق الخلق في ظلمة ثم أفاض عليهم من نوره» وقال: «إن لله ملائكة هم أعلم بأعمال الناس منهم».

(٣١) والأنبياء إذا بلغ معراجهم المبلغ الأقصى وأشرفوا منه إلى السفل ونظروا من فوق إلى تحت اطلعوا أيضاً على قلوب العباد وأشرفوا على جملة من علوم الغيب: إذ من كان في عالم الملكوت كان عند الله تعالى — «وعنده مفاتح الغيب» — أى من عنده تنزل أسباب الموجودات في عالم الشهادة؛ وعالم الشهادة أثر من آثار ذلك العالم، يجرى منه مجرى الظل بالإضافة إلى الشخص، ومجرى الثمرة بالإضافة إلى المثمر، والمسبب بالإضافة إلى السبب. ومفاتيح معرفة المسببات لا توجد إلا من الأسباب: ولذلك كان عالم الشهادة مثالاً لعالم الملكوت كما سيأتي في بيان المشكاة والمصباح والشجرة: لأن المسبب لا يخلو عن موازاة السبب ومحاكاته نوعاً من المحاكاة على قرب أو على بعد. وهذا لأن له غوْراً عميقاً. ومن اطلع على كنه حقيقته انكشف له حقائق أمثلة القرآن على يسر.

دقيقة ترجع إلى حقيقة النور

(٣٢) فنقول إن كان ما يبصر نفسه وغيره أولى باسم النور، فإن كان من جملة ما يبصره غيرُه أيضاً مع أنه يبصر نفسه وغيره، فهو أولى باسم النور من

"light" than that which has no effect at all on others. Or rather, it is more appropriate that it should be called a "light-giving lamp," since it pours forth its light upon other things. This characteristic is found in the holy prophetic spirit, because it is through this spirit that many types of knowledge are poured forth upon creatures. Hence, we understand the meaning of God's naming Muḥammad a "light-giving lamp" [33:46]. All the prophets are lamps, and so are the *ʿulamāʾ*, but the disparity between them is beyond reckoning.

A fine point

(33) If it is proper to call that from which the light of vision comes a "light-giving lamp," then it is appropriate to allude to that by which the lamp itself is kindled as fire. Hence, these earthly lamps originally become kindled only from the high lights. As for the holy prophetic spirit, "its oil well-nigh would shine, even if no fire touched it," but it only becomes "light upon light" [24:35] when touched by fire.

(34) It is appropriate that the place from which the earthly spirits are kindled be [called] the high divine spirit that has been described by ʿAlī and Ibn ʿAbbās—God be pleased with them—both of whom said, "God has an angel who has seventy thousand faces; in every face are seventy thousand tongues, through all of which he glorifies God." It is this angel who stands before all the other angels, for it is said that the day of resurrection is "the day when the Spirit and the angels stand in ranks" [78:38]. When this Spirit is viewed in respect to the fact that the earthly lamps are kindled from it, then the only similitude that this Spirit can have is "fire." And one can only become intimate with this fire "on the side of the Mount" [28:29].[11]

A fine point

(35) If the heavenly lights from which the earthly lights become kindled

الذى لا يؤثر في غيره أصلاً، بل بالحرِىّ أن يسمى سراجاً منيراً لفيضان أنواره على غيره. وهذه الخاصية توجد للروح القدسى النبوى إذ تفيض بواسطتهأنواع المعارف على الخلائق. وبهذا نفهم معنى تسمية الله محمداً عليه السلام سراجاً منيراً. والأنبياء كلهم سُرُج، وكذلك العلماء، ولكن التفاوت بينهم لا يحصى.

دقيقة

(٣٣) إذا كان اللائق بالذى يستفاد منه نور الإبصار أن يسمى سراجاً منيراً فالذى يقتبس منه السراج في نفسه جدير بأن يكنى عنه بالنار. وهذه السرج الأرضية إنما تقتبس في أصلها من أنوار علوية. فالروح القدسى النبوى يكاد زيته يضىء ولو لم تمسسه نار. ولكن إنما يصير نوراً على نور إذا مسته النار.

(٣٤) وبالحرِىّ أن يكون مقتَبَس الأرواح الأرضية هى الروح الإلهية العلوية التى وصفها على وابن عباس رضى الله عنهما فقالا: «إن لله ملَكاً له سبعون ألف وجه في كل وجه سبعون ألف لسان يسبح الله بجميعها» وهو الذى قوبل بالملائكة كلهم فقيل يوم القيامة «يوم يقوم الروح والملائكة صفاً» فهى إذا اعتبرت من حيث يقتبس منها السّرُج الأرضية لم يكن لها مثال إلا النار، وذلك لا يؤانس إلا من جانب الطور.

دقيقة

(٣٥) الأنوار السماوية التى تقتبس منها الأنوار الأرضية إن كان لها ترتيب

have a hierarchy such that one light kindles another, then the light nearest to the First Source is more worthy of the name "light" because it is highest in level. The way to perceive a similitude of this hierarchy in the visible world is to suppose that moonlight enters through a window of a house, falls upon a mirror attached to a wall, is reflected from the mirror to an opposite wall, and turns from that wall to the earth so as to illuminate it. You know that the light on the earth comes from that on the wall, the light on the wall from that on the mirror, the light on the mirror from that in the moon, and the light in the moon from the light in the sun, since light shines from the sun onto the moon. These four lights are ranked in levels such that some are higher and more perfect than others. Each one has a "known station"[12] and a specific degree which it does not overstep.

(36) Know that it has been unveiled to the possessors of insights that the lights of the dominion are likewise only to be found in a hierarchy, and that the light "brought near"[13] is the one that is closest to the Furthest Light. Hence, it is not unlikely that the level of Israfil is above that of Gabriel; that among the angels is one who is the most near because of the nearness of his degree to the Lordly Presence, which is the source of all lights; that among the angels is the furthest; and that between these two are so many degrees that they cannot be counted. The only thing known about these degrees of light is that there are many of them and that their hierarchy derives from their stations and ranks. They are just as they themselves describe, since they have said, "We are those ranged in ranks; we are they that give glory" [37:165–66].[14]

A fine point

(37) Since you have recognized that lights have a hierarchy, know also that this hierarchy does not continue on to infinity. Rather, it climbs to the First Source, which is light in itself and by itself and to which no light comes from any other. From this light all the lights shine forth, according to the hierarchy. Consider now if the name "light" is more appropriate and worthy for that which is illuminated and borrows

بحيث يقتبس بعضها من بعض، فالأقرب من المنبع الأول أولى باسم النور لأنه أعلى رتبة. ومثال ترتيبه في عالم الشهادة لا تدركه إلا بأن يفرض ضوءُ القمر داخلاً في كوة بيت واقعاً على مرآة منصوبة على حائط، ومنعكساً منها إلى حائط آخر في مقابلتها، ثم منعطفاً منه إلى الأرض بحيث تستنير الأرض. فأنت تعلم أن ما على الأرض من النور تابع لما على الحائط وما على الحائط تابع لما على المرآة، وما على المرآة تابع لما في القمر، وما في القمر تابع لما في الشمس: إذ منها يشرق النور على القمر. وهذه الأنوار الأربعة مرتبة بعضها أعلى وأكمل من بعض، ولكل واحد مقام معلوم ودرجة خاصة لا يتعداها.

(٣٦) فاعلم أنه قد انكشف لأرباب البصائر أن الأنوار الملكوتية إنما وجدت على ترتيب كذلك، وأن المقرّب هو الأقرب إلى النور الأقصى. فلا يبعد أن تكون رتبة إسرافيل فوق رتبة جبريل، وأن فيهم الأقرب لقرب درجته من حضرة الربوبية التى هى منبع الأنوار كلها، وأن فيهم الأدنى، وبينهما درجات تستعصى على الإحصاء. وإنما المعلوم كثرتهم وترتيبهم في مقاماتهم وصفوفهم، وأنهم كما وصفوا به أنفسهم إذ قالوا: «وإنا لنحن الصافون. وإنا لنحن المسبحون».

دقيقة

(٣٧) إذا عرفت أن الأنوار لها ترتيب فاعلم أنه لا يتسلسل إلى غير نهاية، بل يرتقى إلى منبع أول هو النور لذاته وبذاته، ليس يأتيه نور من غيره. ومنه تشرق الأنوار كلها على ترتيبها. فانظر الآن اسم النور أحق وأولى بالمستنير

its light from another, or for that which is luminous in itself and which bestows light upon everything else. It seems to me that the truth of this is not hidden from you. Thus, it is verified that the name "light" is more appropriate for the Furthest, Highest Light, beyond which there is no light and from which light descends to others.

A reality

(38) Or rather, I say—without trepidation—that the name "light" for things other than the First Light is a sheer metaphor, since everything other than that Light, when viewed in itself, has no light of its own in respect to its own self. On the contrary, its luminosity is borrowed from another, and this borrowed luminosity is not supported by itself, but rather by another. To attribute a borrowed thing to the one who has borrowed it is sheer metaphor. Do you think that someone who borrows clothing, a horse, a blanket, and a saddle, and who rides the horse when the lender lets him do so and [only] to the extent that he allows is truly rich, or [just] metaphorically so? Is the lender rich or the borrower? It is obvious! In himself the borrower is poor, just as he always was. The only one who is rich is the lender, from whom come loans and gifts and to whom things are returned and taken back.

(39) So the Real Light is He in whose hand is "the creation and the command" [7:54] and from whom illumination comes in the first place and by whom it is preserved in the second place. No one is a partner with Him in the reality of this name, nor in being worthy for it, unless He should name him by it and show him kindness by naming him so, like a master who shows kindness to his slave by giving him property and then calling him a master. When the reality is unveiled to the slave, he knows that he himself and his property belong only to his master, who, of course, has no partner whatsoever in any of this.

المستعير نوره من غيره، أو بالنّير في ذاته المنير لكل ما سواه؟ فما عندى أنه يخفى عليك الحق فيه. وبه يتحقق أن اسم النور أحق بالنور الأقصى الأعلى الذى لا نور فوقه، ومنه ينزل النور إلى غيره.

حقيقة

(٣٨) بل أقول ولا أبالى إن اسم النور على غير النور الأول مجاز محض: إذ كل ما سواه إذا اعتبر ذاته فهو في ذاته من حيث ذاته لا نور له: بل نورانيته مستعارة من غيره ولا قوام لنورانيته المستعارة بنفسها، بل بغيرها. ونسبة المستعار إلى المستعير مجاز محض. أفَتَرَى أن من استعار ثياباً وفرساً ومركباً وسرجاً، وركبه في الوقت الذى أركبه المُعِير، وعلى الحد الذى رسمه، غنى بالحقيقة أو بالمجاز؟ وأن المعير هو الغنى أو المستعير؟ كلا، بل المستعير فقير في نفسه كما كان. وإنما الغنى هو المعير الذى منه الإعارة والإعطاء، وإليه الاسترداد والانتزاع.

(٣٩) فإذن النور الحق هو الذى بيده الخلق والأمر، ومنه الإنارة أولاً والإدامة ثانياً. فلا شركة لأحد معه في حقيقة هذا الاسم ولا في استحقاقه إلا من حيث يسميه به ويتفضل عليه بتسميته تفضل المالك على عبده إذا أعطاه مالاً ثم سماه مالكاً. وإذا انكشف للعبد الحقيقة علم أنه وماله لمالكه على التفرد لا شريك له فيه أصلاً والبتة.

A reality

(40) Now that you recognize that light goes back to manifestation, to making manifest, and to its various levels, you should know that there is no darkness more intense than the concealment of nonexistence. For something dark is called "dark" because sight cannot reach it, so it does not become an existent thing for the observer, even though it exists in itself. How can that which does not exist for others or for itself not be worthy of being the utmost degree of darkness while it stands opposite to existence, which is light? After all, something that is not manifest in itself does not become manifest to others.

(41) Existence can be classified into the existence that a thing possesses in itself and that which it possesses from another. When a thing has existence from another, its existence is borrowed and has no support in itself. When the thing is viewed in itself and with respect to itself, it is pure nonexistence. It only exists inasmuch as it is ascribed to another. This is not a true existence, just as you came to know in the example of the borrowing of clothing and wealth. Hence the Real Existent is God, just as the Real Light is He.

The Reality of realities

(42) From here the gnostics climb from the lowlands of metaphor to the highlands of reality, and they perfect their ascent. Then they see—witnessing with their own eyes—that there is none in existence save God and that "Everything is perishing except His face" [28:88]. [It is] not that each thing is perishing at one time or at other times, but that it is perishing from eternity without beginning to eternity without end. It can only be so conceived since, when the essence of anything other than He is considered in respect of its own essence, it is sheer nonexistence. But when it is viewed in respect of the "face" to which existence flows forth from the First, the Real, then it is seen as existing not in itself but through the face adjacent to its Giver of Existence. Hence, the only existent is the Face of God.

حقيقة

(٤٠) مهما عرفت أن النور يرجع إلى الظهور والإظهار ومراتبه، فاعلم أنه لا ظلمة أشد من كتم العدم: لأن المظلم سمى مظلماً لأنه ليس للإبصار إليه وصول، إذ ليس يصير موجوداً للبصير مع أنه موجود في نفسه. فالذى ليس موجوداً لا لغيره ولا لنفسه كيف لا يستحق أن يكون هو الغاية في الظلمة وفي مقابلته الوجود فهو النور؟: فإن الشىء مالم يظهر في ذاته لا يظهر لغيره.

(٤١) والوجود ينقسم إلى ما للشىء من ذاته وإلى ماله من غيره. وماله الوجود من غيره فوجوده مستعار لا قوام له بنفسه. بل إذا اعتُبر ذاته من حيث ذاته فهو عدم محض. وإنما هو موجود من حيث نسبته إلى غيره، وذلك ليس بوجود حقيقى كما عرفت في مثال استعارة الثوب والغنى. فالموجود الحق هو الله تعالى، كما أن النور الحق هو الله تعالى.

حقيقة الحقائق

(٤٢) من هنا ترقى العارفون من حضيض المجاز إلى يفاع الحقيقة، واستكملوا معراجهم فرأوا بالمشاهدة العيانية أن ليس في الوجود إلا الله تعالى، وأن «كل شىء هالك إلا وجهه» لا أنه يصير هالكاً في وقت من الأوقات؛ بل هو هالك أزلاً وأبداً لا يتصور إلا كذلك؛ فإن كل شىء سواه إذا اعتُبِر ذاته من حيث ذاته فهو عدم محض؛ وإذا اعتبر من الوجه الذى يسرى إليه الوجود من الأول الحق رؤى موجوداً لا في ذاته لكن من الوجه الذى يلى موجده، فيكون الموجود وجه الله تعالى فقط.

(43) Each thing has two faces: a face toward itself, and a face toward its Lord. Viewed in terms of the face of itself, it is nonexistent; but viewed in terms of the face of God, it exists. Hence, nothing exists but God and His face: "Everything is perishing except His face" from eternity without beginning to eternity without end.

(44) The gnostics do not need the day of resurrection to hear the Fashioner proclaim, "Whose is the Kingdom today? God's, the One, the Overwhelming" [40:16]. Rather, this proclamation never leaves their hearing. They do not understand the saying "God is most great" to mean that He is greater than other things. God forbid! After all, there is nothing in existence along with Him that He could be greater than. Or rather, nothing other than He possesses the level of "with-ness";[15] everything possesses the level of following. Indeed, everything other than God exists only with respect to the face adjacent to Him. The only existent thing is His Face. It is absurd to say that God is greater than His Face. Rather, the meaning of "God is most great" is to say that God is too great for any relation or comparison. He is too great for anyone other than He—whether it be a prophet or an angel—to perceive the innermost meaning of His magnificence. Rather, none knows God with innermost knowledge save God. Or rather, every object of knowledge enters the power and mastery of the gnostic only after a fashion. Otherwise, that would contradict God's majesty and magnificence. This can be verified, as we mentioned, in the book *Al-maqṣad al-asnā fī sharḥ maᶜānī asmāʾ Allāh al-ḥusnā* [The highest goal in the meanings of God's most beautiful names].[16]

An allusion

(45) The gnostics, after having ascended to the heaven of reality, agree that they see nothing in existence save the One, the Real. Some of them possess this state as a cognitive gnosis. Others, however, attain this through a state of tasting. Plurality is totally banished from them, and they become immersed in sheer singularity. Their rational faculties become so satiated that in this state they are, as it were, stunned. No room remains in them for the remembrance of any other than God, nor the remembrance of themselves. Nothing is with them but God. They

(٤٣) فلكل شىء وجهان: وجه إلى نفسه ووجه إلى ربه؛ فهو باعتبار وجه نفسه عدم وباعتبار وجه الله تعالى موجود. فإذن لا موجود إلا الله تعالى ووجهه. فإذن كل شىء هالك إلا وجهه أزلاً وأبداً.

(٤٤) ولم يفتقر هؤلاء إلى يوم القيامة ليسمعوا نداء البارى تعالى «لمن الملك اليوم؟ لله الواحد القهار». بل هذا النداء لا يفارق سمعهم أبداً. ولم يفهموا من معنى قوله «الله أكبر» أنه أكبر من غيره، حاش لله، إذ ليس في الوجود معه غيره حتى يكون أكبر منه؛ بل ليس لغيره رتبة المعية، بل رتبة التبعية. بل ليس لغيره وجود إلا من الوجه الذى يليه. فالموجود وجهه فقط. ومحال أن يقال إنه أكبر من وجهه. بل معناها أنه أكبر من أن يقال له أكبر بمعنى الإضافة والمقايسة، وأكبر من أن يدرك غيره كنه كبريائه، نبياً كان أو مَلَكاً. بل لا يعرف الله كنه معرفته إلا الله. بل كل معروف داخل في سلطة العارف واستيلائه دخولاً مّا؛ وذلك ينافي الجلال والكبرياء. وهذا له تحقيق ذكرناه في كتاب «المقصد الأسنى في معانى أسماء الله الحسنى».

إشارة

(٤٥) العارفون—بعد العروج إلى سماء الحقيقة—اتفقوا على أنهم لم يروا في الوجود إلا الواحد الحق. لكن منهم من كان له هذه الحال عرفاناً علمياً، ومنهم من صار له ذلك حالاً ذوقياً. وانتفت عنهم الكثرة بالكلية واستغرقوا بالفردانية المحضة واستوفيت فيها عقولهم فصاروا كالمبهوتين فيه ولم يبق فيهم متسع لا لذكر غير الله ولا لذكر أنفسهم أيضاً. فلم يكن عندهم إلا الله،

become intoxicated with such an intoxication that the ruling authority of their rational faculty is overthrown. Hence, one of them says, "I am the Real!" another, "Glory be to me, how great is my station!" and still another, "There is nothing in my robe but God!"[17]

(46) The speech of lovers in the state of intoxication should be concealed and not spread about. When this intoxication subsides, the ruling authority of the rational faculty—which is God's balance in His earth—is given back to them. They come to know that what they experienced was not the reality of unification[18] but that it was similar to unification. It was like the words of the lover during a state of extreme passionate love:

> I am He whom I love,
> and He whom I love is I![19]

(47) It is not unlikely that a person could look into a mirror in an unexpected place and not see the mirror at all. He supposes that the form he sees is the mirror's form and that it is united with the mirror. Likewise, he could see wine in a glass and suppose that the wine is the glass's color. When the situation becomes familiar to him and his foot becomes firmly established within it, he asks for forgiveness from God and says:

> The glass is clear, the wine is clear,
> the two are similar, the affair confused,
> As if there is wine and no glass,
> or glass and no wine.[20]

There is a difference between saying "The wine is the cup" and "It is *as if* the wine is the cup."

(48) When this state gets the upper hand, it is called "extinction" in relation to the one who possesses it. Or, rather, it is called "extinction from extinction," since the possessor of the state is extinct from himself and from his own extinction. For he is conscious neither of himself in that state, nor of his own unconsciousness of himself. If he were conscious of his own unconsciousness, then he would [still] be conscious of himself. In relation to the one immersed in it, this state is called "unification," according to the language of metaphor, or is called "declaring God's unity," according to the language of reality. And behind these realities there are also mysteries, but it would take too long to delve into them.

فسكروا سكراً دفع دونه سلطان عقولهم، فقال أحدهم «أنا الحق» وقال الآخر «سبحانى ما أعظم شانى!» وقال آخر «ما في الجبة إلا الله».

(٤٦) وكلام العشاق في حال السكر يُطوَى ولا يحكى. فلما خف عنهم سكرهم وردوا إلى سلطان العقل الذى هو ميزان الله في أرضه، عرفوا أن ذلك لم يكن حقيقة الاتحاد بل شبه الاتحاد مثل قول العاشق في حال فرط عشقه «أنا من أهوى ومن أهوى أنا»

(٤٧) ولا يبعد أن يفاجىء الإنسان مرآةً فينظر فيها ولم ير المرآة قط، فيظن أن الصورة التى رآها هى صورة المرآة متحدة بها، ويرى الخمر في الزجاج فيظن أن الخمر لون الزجاج. وإذا صار ذلك عنده مألوفاً ورسخ فيه قدمه استغفر وقال:

رق الزجاج وراقت الخمر فتشابها فتشاكل الأمر
فكأنما خمر ولا قدح وكأنما قدح ولا خمر

وفرق بين أن يقول: الخمر قدح، وبين أن يقول: كأنه قدح.

(٤٨) وهذه الحالة إذا غلبت سميت بالإضافة إلى صاحب الحالة «فناء»، بل «فناء الفناء» : لأنه فنى عن نفسه وفنى عن فنائه، فإنه ليس يشعر بنفسه في تلك الحال ولا بعدم شعوره بنفسه. ولو شعر بعدم شعوره بنفسه لكان قد شعر بنفسه، وتسمى هذه الحالة بالإضافة إلى المستغرق به بلسان المجاز اتحاداً أو بلسان الحقيقة توحيداً. ووراء هذه الحقائق أيضاً أسرار يطول الخوض فيها.

Conclusion

(49) Perhaps you desire to know the manner in which God's light is ascribed to the heavens and the earth—or, rather, the manner in which God is the light of the heavens and the earth in His own essence. It is not appropriate to keep this knowledge hidden from you, since you already know that God is light, that there is no light other than He, and that He is the totality of lights and the Universal Light. This is because the word "light" is an expression for that through which things are unveiled; in a higher sense, it is that through which and for which things are unveiled; in a still higher sense, it is that through which, for which, and by which things are unveiled. Then, in the true sense, light is that through which, for which, and by which things are unveiled and beyond which there is no light from which this light could be kindled and take replenishment. Rather, it possesses light in itself, from itself, and for itself, not from another. Moreover, you know that only the First Light has these qualities.

(50) In addition, you know that the heavens and the earth are filled with light from the two levels of light: that is, the light ascribed to eyesight and [the light ascribed] to insight; or, in other words, [light ascribed] to the senses and to the rational faculty. As for the light ascribed to eyesight, that [light] is the stars, the sun, and the moon that we see in the heavens, and their rays that are deployed over everything on the earth that we see. Through [this light] the diverse colors become manifest, especially in springtime. This light is also deployed over every situation of the animals, minerals, and all types of existent things. Were it not for these rays, colors would have no manifestation—or, rather, no existence; and all shapes and measures that become manifest to the senses are perceived by the function of colors. The perception of colors is inconceivable without these rays.

(51) As for the suprasensory, rational lights, the higher world is filled with them; they are the substances of the angels. The lower world is also filled with them; they are animal life and human life. Through the low, human light, the proper order of the world of lowness becomes manifest, just as through the angelic light the proper order of the world of highness becomes manifest. This is what God means by His words: "He configured you from the earth and has given you to live therein" [11:61]. He also said,

خاتمة

(٤٩) لعلك تشتهى أن تعرف وجه إضافة نوره إلى السموات والأرض؛ بل وجه كونه في ذاته نور السموات والأرض، فلا ينبغى أن يخفى ذلك عليك بعد أن عرفت أنه النور ولا نور سواه وأنه كل الأنوار، وأنه النور الكلى، لأن النور عبارة عما ينكشف به الأشياء، وأعلى منه ما ينكشف به وله، وأعلى منه ما ينكشف به وله ومنه، وأن الحقيق منه ما ينكشف به وله ومنه وليس فوقه نور منه اقتباسه واستمداده: بل ذلك له في ذاته من ذاته لذاته لا من غيره. ثم عرفت أن هذا لن يتصف به إلا النور الأول.

(٥٠) ثم عرفت أن السموات والأرض مشحونة نوراً من طبقتى النور: أعنى المنسوب إلى البصر والبصيرة: أى إلى الحس والعقل. أما البصرى فما نشاهده في السموات من الكواكب والشمس والقمر، وما نشاهده في الأرض من الأشعة المنبسطة على كل ما على الأرض حتى ظهرت به الألوان المختلفة خصوصاً في الربيع، وعلى كل حال في الحيوانات والمعادن وأصناف الموجودات. ولو لاها لم يكن للألوان ظهور، بل وجود. ثم سائر ما يظهر للحس من الأشكال والمقادير يدرَك تبعاً للألوان ولا يتصور إدراكها إلابواسطتها.

(٥١) وأما الأنوار العقلية المعنوية فالعالم الأعلى مشحون بها، وهى جواهر الملائكة، والعالم الأسفل مشحون بها وهى الحياة الحيوانية ثم الإنسانية. وبالنور الإنسانى السفلى ظهر نظام عالم السفل كما بالنور الملكى ظهر نظام عالم العلو. وهو المعنىّ بقوله «أنشأكم من الأرض واستعمركم فيها» وقال تعالى:

"He will surely make you vicegerents in the earth" [24:55]. Again, He said, "And He has appointed you to be vicegerents in the earth" [27:62]. And He said, "I am setting in the earth a vicegerent" [2:30].

(52) Once you have come to know this, you will know that the world in its entirety is filled with both manifest, visual lights and nonmanifest, rational lights. Then you will know the following: The low lights flow forth from one another just as light flows forth from a lamp. The lamp is the holy prophetic spirit. The holy prophetic spirits are kindled from the high spirits, just as a lamp is kindled from a light. Some of the high things kindle each other, and their hierarchy is a hierarchy of stations. Then all of them climb to the Light of lights, their Origin, their First Source. This is God alone, who has no partner. All other lights are borrowed. The only true light is His. Everything is His light—or, rather, He is everything. Or, rather, nothing possesses a "he-ness" other than He, except in a metaphorical sense. Therefore, there is no light except His light.

(53) Other lights are lights derived from the light that is adjacent to Him, not from His own Essence. Thus, the face of every possessor of a face is toward Him and turned in His direction. "Whithersoever you turn, there is the face of God" [2:115]. Hence, there is no god but He. For "god" is an expression for that toward which a face turns through worship and becoming godlike. Here I mean the faces of the hearts, since they are lights. Indeed, just as there is no god but He, so also there is no he but He, because "he" is an expression for whatever may be pointed to, and there is no pointing to anything but Him. Or, rather, whenever you point to something, in reality you are pointing to Him. If you do not know this, that is because you are heedless of "the Reality of realities" that we mentioned.

(54) One does not point to the light of the sun but, rather, to the sun. In the obvious sense of this example, everything in existence is related to God just as light is related to the sun. Therefore, "There is no god but God" is the declaration of God's unity of the common people, while "There is no he but He" is the declaration of God's unity of the elect, since this declaration of God's unity is more complete, more specific, more comprehensive, more worthy, and more precise. It is more able to make its possessor enter into sheer singularity and utter oneness.

«ليستخلفنهم في الأرض» وقال: «ويجعلكم خلفاء الأرض»، وقال: «إني جاعل في الأرض خليفة».

(٥٢) فإذا عرفت هذا عرفت أن العالم بأسره مشحون بالأنوار الظاهرة البصرية والباطنة العقلية، ثم عرفت أن السفلية فائضة بعضها من بعض فيضان النور من السراج وأن السراج هو الروح النبوى القدسى، وأن الأرواح النبوية القدسية مقتبسة من الأرواح العلوية اقتباس السراج من النور؛ وأن العلويات بعضها مقتبسة من البعض، وأن ترتيبها ترتيب مقامات. ثم ترقى جملتها إلى نور الأنوار ومعدنها ومنبعها الأول؛ وأن ذلك هو الله تعالى وحده لا شريك له، وأن سائر الأنوار مستعارة، وإنما الحقيق نوره فقط؛ وأن الكل نوره، بل هو الكل، بل لا هوية لغيره إلا بالمجاز.

(٥٣) فإذن لانور إلانوره، وسائر الأنوار أنوار من الذى يليه لا من ذاته. فوجه كل ذى وجه إليه ومولّ شطره: «فأينما تولوا فثم وجه الله». فإذن لا إله إلا هو: فإن الإله عبارة عما الوجه موليه نحوه بالعبادة والتأله: أعنى وجوه القلوب فإنها الأنوار بل كما لا إله إلا هو، فلا هو إلا هو: لأن «هو» عبارة عما إليه إشارة كيفما كان، ولا إشارة إلا إليه. بل كل ما أشرت إليه فهو بالحقيقة إشارة إليه وإن كنت لا تعرفه أنت لغفلتك عن حقيقة الحقائق التى ذكرناها.

(٥٤) ولا إشارة إلى نور الشمس بل إلى الشمس. فكل ما في الوجود فنسبته إليه في ظاهر المثال كنسبة النور إلى الشمس. فإذن «لا إله إلا الله» توحيد العوام، «ولا إله إلا هو» توحيد الخواص، لأن هذا أتم وأخص وأشمل وأحق وأدق وأدخل بصاحبه في الفردانية المحضة والوحدانية الصرفة.

(55) The final end of the creatures' ascent is the kingdom of singularity. Beyond it, there is no place to climb. Climbing is inconceivable without plurality, since climbing is a sort of relation that demands something away from which one climbs and something toward which one climbs. But when plurality disappears, oneness is actualized, relationships are nullified, and allusions are swept away. There remains neither high nor low, descending nor ascending. Climbing is impossible, so ascent is impossible. Hence, there is no highness beyond the highest, no plurality alongside oneness, and no ascent when plurality is negated. If there is a change of state, it is through descent to the heaven of this world[21]—that is, through viewing the low from the high, since the highest, though it has a lower, does not have a higher.

(56) This is the ultimate of goals and the final end of everything searched for. He who knows it knows it, and he who denies it is ignorant of it. It belongs to the "kind of knowledge which is like the guise of the hidden; none knows it except those who know God. When they speak of it, none denies it except those who are arrogantly deluded about God."[22]

(57) It is not unlikely that the *ʿulamāʾ* will say that "the descent to the heaven of this world" is the descent of an angel, for the *ʿulamāʾ* come up with even more unlikely ideas. For example, one of them says that the person who is drowned in singularity also has a descent to the heaven of this world—namely, his descent to employ his senses or move his limbs. This is alluded to in God's words: "I become the hearing by which he hears, the seeing by which he sees, and the tongue by which he speaks."[23] When He is his hearing, his sight, and his tongue, then He alone hears, sees, and speaks. This is alluded to in His words: "I was sick and you did not visit me,"[24] and so on to the end of the *ḥadīth*. Hence, the movements of this person who has realized God's unity come from the heaven of this world. His sensations, like hearing and seeing, come from a higher heaven, and his rational faculty is above that. He climbs from the heaven of the rational faculty to the utmost degree of the ascent of the creatures. The kingdom of singularity completes the seven levels. Then he sits upon the throne of oneness and from it governs the affair of the levels of his heavens.[25]

(٥٥) ومنتهى معراج الخلائق مملكة الفردانية. وليس وراء ذلك مرقى: إذ الترقي لا يتصور إلا بكثرة: فإنه نوع إضافة يستدعى ما منه الارتقاء وما إليه الارتقاء. وإذا ارتفعت الكثرة حقت الوحدة وبطلت الإضافات وطاحت الإشارات ولم يبق علو وسفل ونازل ومرتفع: واستحال الترقي فاستحال العروج. فليس وراء الأعلى علو، ولا مع الوحدة كثرة، ولا مع انتفاء الكثرة عروج. فإن كان من تغير حال. فالنزول إلى سماء الدنيا: أعنى بالإشراف من علو إلى سفل لأن الأعلى له أسفل وليس له أعلى.

(٥٦) فهذه هى غاية الغايات ومنتهى الطلبات: يعلمه من يعلمه وينكره من يجهله. وهو من العلم الذى هو كهيئة المكنون الذى لا يعلمه إلا العلماء بالله. فإذا نطقوا به لم ينكره إلا أهل الغِرّة بالله.

(٥٧) ولا يبعد أن قال العلماء إن النزول إلى السماء الدنيا هو نزول مَلَك: فقد توهم العلماء ما هو أبعد منه؛ إذ قال هذا المستغرق بالفردانية أيضاً له نزول إلى السماء الدنيا: فإن ذلك هو نزوله إلى استعمال الحواس أو تحريك الأعضاء. وإليه الإشارة بقوله «صرت سمعه الذى يسمع به وبصره الذى يبصر به ولسانه الذى ينطق به». فإذا كان هو سمعه وبصره ولسانه، فهو السامع والباصر والناطق إذن لا غيره؛ وإليه الإشارة بقوله: «مرضت فلم تعدنى» الحديث. فحركات هذا الموحّد من السماء الدنيا، وإحساساته كالسمع والبصر من سماء فوقه، وعقله فوق ذلك. وهو يترقى من سماء العقل إلى منتهى معراج الخلائق. ومملكة الفردانية تمام سبع طبقات ثم بعده يستوى على عرش الوحدانية، ومنه يدبّر الأمر لطبقات سمواته.

(58) It may happen that an observer considering this person will apply the words, "God created Adam upon the form of the All-Merciful," unless he considers carefully and comes to know that this saying has an interpretation, like the words "I am the Real!" and "Glory be to Me!" Or rather, it is like God's words, to Moses, "I was sick and you did not visit Me," and His words, "I am his hearing, his seeing, and his tongue." I think I will hold back from clarification, because I see that you are incapable of bearing anything greater than this.

Some encouragement

(59) Perhaps your aspiration does not rise high enough for these words, but rather falls short below their summit. So take for yourself words that are nearer to your understanding and more suitable to your weakness.

(60) Know that you can come to know the meaning of the fact that God is the light of the heavens and the earth in relation to manifest, visual light. For example, when you see the lights and greenness of springtime in the brightness of day, you do not doubt that you see colors. But you may suppose that you do not see anything along with colors, since you say, "I see nothing with greenness other than greenness." A group of people have insisted on this, since they suppose that light has no meaning and that there is nothing along with colors except colors. Hence, they deny the existence of light, even though it is the most manifest of things. How could it not be? For through it things become manifest. It is light which is seen in itself and through which other things are seen, as was said earlier.

(61) When the sun sets, when lamps are put away, and when shadows fall, the deniers perceive a self-evident distinction between the locus of the shadow and the place of brightness. Hence, they confess that light is a meaning beyond colors that is perceived along with colors. It is as if the intensity of light's disclosure prevents it from being perceived and the intensity of its manifestation keeps it hidden. Manifestation may be the cause of hiddenness. When a thing passes its own limit, it reverts to its opposite.

(٥٨) فربما نظر الناظر إليه فأطلق القول بأن الله خلق آدم على صورة الرحمن، إلى أن يمعن النظر فيعلم أن ذلك له تأويل كقول القائل «أنا الحق» و«سبحانى» بل كقوله لموسى عليه السلام: «مرضت فلم تعدنى» و«كنت سمعه وبصره ولسانه». وأرى الآن قبض البيان فما أراك تطيق من هذا القدْر أكثر من هذا القدْر.

مساعدة

(٥٩) لعلك لاتسمو إلى هذا الكلام بهمتك، بل تقصر دون ذروته همتُك، فخذ إليك كلاماً أقرب إلى فهمك وأوفق لضعفك.

(٦٠) واعلم أن معنى كونه نور السموات والأرض تعرفه بالنسبة إلى النور الظاهر البصرى. فإذا رأيت أنوار الربيع وخضرته مثلاً في ضياء النهار فلست تشك في أنك ترى الألوان. وربما ظننت أنك لست ترى مع الألوان غيرها، فإنك تقول لست أرى مع الخضرة غير الخضرة. ولقد أصر على هذا قوم فزعموا أن النور لا معنى له، وأنه ليس مع الألوان غير الألوان، فأنكروا وجود النور مع أنه أظهر الأشياء، وكيف لا وبه تظهر الأشياء، وهو الذى يبصَر في نفسه ويبصَر به غيره كما سبق.

(٦١) لكن عند غروب الشمس وغيبة السراج ووقوع الظل أدركوا تفرقة ضرورية بين محل الظل وبين موقع الضياء فاعترفوا بأن النور معنى وراء الألوان يدرك مع الألوان حتى كأنه لشدة انجلائه لا يدرك، ولشدة ظهوره يخفى. وقد يكون الظهور سبب الخفاء. والشيء إذا جاوز حده انعكس على ضده.

(62) Now that you have recognized this, you should know that the masters of insight never see a thing without seeing God along with it. One of them might add to this and say, "I never see a thing without seeing God before it."[26] This is because one of them may see things through God, while another may see the things and see Him through the things. Allusion to the first is made by His words, "Suffices it not as to thy Lord, that He is witness over everything?" [41:53]. Allusion to the second is made with His words, "We will show them Our signs in the horizons" [41:53]. The first is a possessor of witnessing, while the second is a possessor of conclusions that he draws about Him. The first is the degree of the righteous,[27] while the second is the degree of those firmly rooted in knowledge. There is nothing after these two except the degree of those who are heedless and veiled.

(63) Now that you have recognized this, you should know that just as everything becomes manifest to eyesight through outward light, so also everything becomes manifest to inward insight through God. God is with everything and not separate from it. Then He makes everything manifest. In the same way, light is with all things, and through it they become manifest. But here a difference remains: It is conceivable that outward light may disappear through the setting of the sun. It becomes veiled so that shadow appears. As for the divine light through which everything becomes manifest, its disappearance is inconceivable. Or, rather, it is impossible for it to change, so it remains perpetually with the things.

(64) Thus, the way of drawing conclusions about God through separation is cut off. If we suppose that God's light were to disappear, then the heavens and the earth would be destroyed. Because of this separation, something would be perceived that would force one to recognize that it makes things manifest. But since all things are exactly the same in testifying to the oneness of their Creator, differences disappear and the way becomes hidden.

(65) The obvious way to reach knowledge of things is through opposites. But when something neither changes nor has opposites, all states are alike in giving witness to it. Hence, it is not unreasonable that God's light be hidden, that its hiddenness derive from the intensity of its disclosure,

(٦٢) فإذا عرفت هذا فاعلم أن أرباب البصائر ما رأوا شيئاً إلا رأوا الله معه. وربما زاد على هذا بعضهم فقال «ما رأيت شيئاً إلا رأيت الله قبله» لأن منهم من يرى الأشياء به. ومنهم من يرى الأشياء فيراه بالأشياء. وإلى الأول الإشارة بقوله تعالى: «أو لم يكف بربك أنه على كل شيء شهيد»؛ وإلى الثانى الإشارة بقوله تعالى: «سنريهم آياتنا في الآفاق» فالأول صاحب مشاهدة، والثانى صاحب الاستدلال عليه. والأول درجة الصديقين، والثانى درجة العلماء الراسخين، وليس بعدهما إلا درجة الغافلين المحجوبين.

(٦٣) وإذ قد عرفت هذا فاعلم أنه كما ظهر كل شيء للبصر بالنور الظاهر، فقد ظهر كل شيء للبصيرة الباطنة بالله. فهو مع كل شيء لا يفارقه ثم يظهر كل شيء، كما أن النور مع كل شيء وبه يظهر. ولكن بقى ها هنا تفاوت: وهو أن النور الظاهر يُتَصور أن يغيب بغروب الشمس ويحجب حتى يظهر الظل، وأما النور الإلهى الذى به يظهر كل شيء، لا يتصور غيبته بل يستحيل تغيره. فيبقى مع الأشياء دائماً.

(٦٤) فانقطع طريق الاستدلال بالتفرقة. ولو تصوّر غيبته لانهدت السموات والأرض، ولأدرك به من التفرقة ما يضطر معه إلى المعرفة بما به ظهرت الأشياء. ولكن لما تساوت الأشياء كلها على نمط واحد في الشهادة على وحدانية خالقها ارتفع التفريق وخفى الطريق.

(٦٥) إذ الطريق الظاهر معرفة الأشياء بالأضداد؛ فما لا ضد له ولا تغير له تتشابه الأحوال في الشهادة له. فلا يبعد أن يخفى ويكون خفاؤه لشدة جلائه

and that heedlessness of it stems from the radiance of its brightness. So glory be to Him who is hidden from creatures through the intensity of His manifestation and veiled from them because of the radiance of His light!

(66) It may be that some people will fall short of understanding the innermost meaning of these words. Hence, they will understand our words, "God is with everything, just as light is with the things," to mean that He is in each place—high exalted and holy is He from being ascribed to place! Probably the best way not to stir up such imaginings is to say that He is before everything, that He is above everything, and that He makes everything manifest. Yet, in the knowledge of those who possess insight, that which makes manifest cannot be separate from that which is made manifest. This is what we mean by our saying that "He is with everything." Moreover, it is not hidden from you that the manifester is above and before everything made manifest, although it is with everything in a certain respect. However, [the manifester] is with [everything] in one respect and before it in another respect, so you should not suppose that this is a contradiction. Take an example from sensory objects, which lie at your level of knowledge: Consider how the movement of a hand is both with the movement of its shadow and before it. He whose breast cannot embrace knowledge of this should abandon this type of science. There are men for every science, and "the way is eased for each person to that for which he was created."[28]

والغفلة عنه لإشراق ضيائه. فسبحان من اختفى عن الخلق لشدة ظهوره، واحتجب عنهم لإشراق نوره.

(٦٦) وربما لم يفهم أيضاً كنه هذا الكلام بعض القاصرين، فيفهم من قولنا «إن الله مع كل شىء كالنور مع الأشياء» أنه في كل مكان؛ تعالى وتقدس عن النسبة إلى المكان. بل لعل الأبعد عن إثارة هذا الخيال أن نقول إنه قبل كل شىء؛ وإنه فوق كل شىء؛ وإنه مُظِهر كل شىء. والمظهِر لا يفارق المظهَر في معرفة صاحب البصيرة. فهو الذى نعنى بقولنا إنه مع كل شىء. ثم لا يخفى عليك أيضاً أن المظهِر قبل المظهَر وفوقه مع أنه معه بوجه: لكنه معه بوجه وقبله بوجه. فلا تظنن أنه متناقض، واعتبر بالمحسوسات التى هى درجتك في العرفان؛ وانظر كيف تكون حركة اليد مع حركة ظل اليد وقبلها أيضاً. ومن لم يتسع صدره لمعرفة هذا فليهجر هذا النمط من العلم، فلكل علم رجال؛ «وكلّ ميسّر لما خلق له.»

The Second Chapter

Clarifying the similitude of the niche, the lamp, the glass, the tree, the olive, and the fire

(1) True knowledge of this calls for presenting two poles, the area between which has no defined limit. I will allude to them briefly through symbols.

(2) The first pole clarifies the mystery and the method of using similitudes; the respect in which the spirits of the meanings are grasped within the frames of the similitudes; how an interrelationship is established between similitudes and meanings; and how there is a parallel between the visible world (from which the clay of the similitudes is taken) and the world of dominion (from which the spirits of the meanings descend).

(3) The second pole concerns the layers of the spirits of the human clay, and the levels of their lights—since this similitude [of the niche and so forth] was put forth in order to clarify these [layers and levels]. Thus Ibn Mas^{c}ūd reads [the Light Verse and says:] "The similitude of His light in the heart of one who has faith is like a niche," and Ubayy ibn Ka^{c}b reads [it and says:] "The similitude of light is of the heart of one who has faith."

The first pole

Concerning the mystery and method of using similitudes

(4) Know that the cosmos is two worlds: spiritual and bodily. If you want, you can say "sensory and rational," or "high and low." All these words are close in meaning. They differ only through different viewpoints.

الفصل الثانى

في بيان مثال المشكاة والمصباح والزجاجة والشجرة والزيت والنار

(١) ومعرفة هذا يستدعى تقديم قطبين يتسع المجال فيهما إلى غير حد محدود. لكنى أشير إليهما بالرمز والاختصار:

(٢) أحدهما في بيان سر التمثيل ومنهاجه ووجه ضبط أرواح المعانى بقوالب الأمثلة، ووجه كيفية المناسبة بينها، وكيفية الموازنة بين عالم الشهادة التى منها تتخذ طينة الأمثال، وعالم الملكوت الذى منه تستنزل أرواح المعانى.

(٣) والثانى في طبقات أرواح الطينة البشرية ومراتب أنوارها؛ فإن هذا المثال مسوق لبيان ذلك؛ إذ قرأ ابن مسعود «مثل نوره في قلب المؤمن كمشكاة» وقرأ أُبَىّ بن كعب: «مثل نور قلب من آمن»

القطب الأول

فى سر التمثيل ومنهاجه

(٤) اعلم أن العالم عالمان: روحانى وجسمانى: وإن شئت قلت: حِسى وعقلى؛ وإن شئت علوى وسفلى. والكل متقارب، وإنما تختلف باختلاف

Hence, when you view the two worlds in themselves, you will say "bodily and spiritual." When you view them in relation to the eye that perceives them, you will say "sensory and rational." When you view them in relation to one another, you will say "high and low."

(5) It may happen that you name one of these worlds "the world of the kingdom and the visible," while the other is the "unseen world and the dominion."[1] One who considers the realities of these words may become bewildered by the multiplicity of the words and imagine many meanings. But one to whom the realities are unveiled will make the meaning a root and the words a follower. This situation is reversed in the weak, since they search for the realities from the words. God alludes to these two groups with His words, "What, is he who walks prone upon his face better guided, or he who walks upright on a straight path?" [67:22].

(6) Now that you have come to know the meaning of the two worlds, know that the world of dominion is an unseen world, since it is concealed from the majority, while the sensory world is a visible world, since everyone witnesses it. The sensory world is a ladder to the rational world, for, if there were no connection and relationship between the two, the way of climbing to the rational world would be blocked. If climbing were impossible, travel to the presence of lordship and nearness to God would also be impossible.

(7) No one comes near to God unless he steps into the midst of the enclosure of holiness. What we mean by the world of "holiness" is the world that is elevated beyond the perception of the senses and the imagination. If we view its totality such that nothing leaves it and such that what is foreign to it does not enter it, then we call it the "enclosure of holiness." It may happen that we name the human spirit, which is a channel for the flashes of holiness, "the holy riverbed" [20:12]. Then there are other enclosures in this enclosure, some of which are more intensely devoted to the meanings of holiness. But the word "enclosure" encompasses all its layers. So do not suppose that these words are irrational ravings to those who possess insights.

الاعتبارات: فإذا اعتبرتهما في أنفسهما قلت جسمانى وروحانى، وإن اعتبرتهما بالإضافة إلى العين المدركة لهما قلت حسى وعقلى. وإن اعتبرتهما بإضافة أحدهما إلى الآخر قلت علوى وسفلى.

(٥) وربما سميت أحدهما عالم الملك والشهادة والآخر عالم الغيب والملكوت. ومن نظر إلى الحقائق من الألفاظ ربما تحير عند كثرة الألفاظ تخيّل كثرة المعانى. والذى تنكشف له الحقائق يجعل المعانى أصلاً والألفاظ تابعاً. وأمر الضعيف بالعكس؛ إذ يطلب الحقائق من الألفاظ. وإلى الفريقين الإشارة بقوله تعالى: «أفمن يمشى مكباً على وجهه أهدى أم من يمشى سوياً على صراط مستقيم»؟

(٦) وإذ قد عرفت معنى العالَمين فاعلم أن العالم الملكوتى عالم غيب؛ إذ هو غائب عن الأكثرين. والعالم الحسى عالم شهادة إذ يشهده الكافة. والعالم الحسى مرقاة إلى العقلى. فلو لم يكن بينهما اتصال ومناسبة لانسدّ طريق الترقي إليه. ولو تعذر ذلك لتعذر السفر إلى حضرة الربوبية والقرب من الله تعالى.

(٧) فلم يقرب من الله تعالى أحد ما لم يطأ بحبوحة حظيرة القدس. والعالم المرتفع عن إدراك الحس والخيال هو الذى نعنيه بعالم القدس. فإذا اعتبرنا جملته بحيث لا يخرج منه شيء ولا يدخل فيه ما هو غريب منه سميناه حظيرة القدس. وربما سمينا الروح البشرى الذى هو مجرى لوائح القدس «الوادى المقدس». ثم هذه الحظيرة فيها حظائر بعضها أشد إمعاناً في معانى القدس. ولكن لفظ الحظيرة يحيط بجميع طبقاتها. فلا تظنن أن هذه الألفاظ طامات غير معقولة عند أرباب البصائر

(8) My occupation just now with explaining every term that I mentioned has hindered me in my goal. You should undertake to understand these words. Let me return to my objective. I say:

(9) The visible world is a ladder to the world of dominion, and traveling on the "straight path" [1:6] consists of climbing this ladder. One may refer to this traveling as "religion" and the "waystations of guidance." If there were no relationship and connection between the two worlds, climbing from one world to the other would be inconceivable. Hence, the divine mercy made the visible world parallel to the world of dominion; there is nothing in this world that is not a similitude of something in the world of dominion.

(10) It may be that one thing [in the visible world] is a similitude for many things in the world of dominion, and that one thing in the world of dominion has many similitudes in the visible world. A thing is only a similitude when it is like and corresponds to something by virtue of a certain kind of likeness and correspondence. To enumerate all these similitudes would call for an exhaustive study of the totality of the existent things found in both worlds in their entirety. Human strength is inadequate for such a study and cannot understand it, since short lifetimes are insufficient to explain it. The most I can do is acquaint you with an example. Then, from the few, you may draw conclusions concerning the many, and the gate of seeking an interpretation of these types of mysteries may be opened for you. Thus, I say:

(11) There are in the world of dominion noble and high luminous substances called "angels." Lights effuse from these angels upon human spirits, and because of these lights these angels may be called "lords"—that is why God is "Lord of the lords." These angels have diverse levels in their luminosity. Hence, it is appropriate for their similitude in the visible world to be the sun, the moon, and the stars.

(٨) واشتغالى الآن بشرح كل لفظ مع ذكره يصدنى عن المقصد. فعليك التشمير لفهم هذه الألفاظ. فأرجع إلى الغرض وأقول:

(٩) لما كان عالم الشهادة مرقاة إلى عالم الملكوت، وكان سلوك الصراط المستقيم عبارة عن هذا الترقي؛ وقد يعبر عنه بالدين وبمنازل الهدى. فلو لم يكن بينهما مناسبة واتصال لما تصور الترقي من أحدهما إلى الآخر. جعلت الرحمة الإلهية عالم الشهادة على موازنة عالم الملكوت: فما من شيء من هذا العالم إلا وهو مثال لشيء من ذلك العالم.

(١٠) وربما كان الشيء الواحد مثالاً لأشياء من عالم الملكوت. وربما كان للشيء الواحد من الملكوت أمثلة كثيرة من عالم الشهادة. وإنما يكون مثالاً إذا ماثله نوعاً من المماثلة، وطابقه نوعاً من المطابقة. وإحصاء تلك الأمثلة يستدعى استقصاء جميع موجودات العالمين بأسرها، ولن تفى به القوة البشرية وما اتسع لفهمه القوة البشرية. فلا تفى بشرحه الأعمار القصيرة. فغايتى أن أعرّفك منها أنموذجاً لتستدل باليسير منها على الكثير، وينفتح لك باب الاستعبار بهذا النمط من الأسرار فأقول:

(١١) إن كان في عالم الملكوت جواهر نورانية شريفة عالية يعبّر عنها بالملائكة، منها تفيض الأنوار على الأرواح البشرية، ولأجلها قد تسمى أرباباً، ويكون الله تعالى رب الأرباب لذلك، ويكون لها مراتب في نورانيتها متفاوتة، فبالحرِيّ أن يكون مثالها من عالم الشهادة الشمس والقمر والكواكب.

(12) The traveler on the path first reaches the angel whose degree is the degree of the stars. The radiance of its light becomes clear to him. The truth becomes unveiled to him that the lower world is completely under its ruling authority and its light's radiance. Because of its beauty and the highness of its degree, something occurs to him and he says, "This is my Lord!" [6:76].

(13) Then, when that which is higher—that whose level is the level of the moon—becomes clear to him, he sees the first enter the setting place of falling down in relation to what is above it. Thus, he says, "I love not the setters" [6:76].

(14) In the same way, he keeps on climbing until he reaches that angel whose similitude is the sun. He sees it to be greater and higher. He sees that it is receptive to the similitude because it has a certain kind of relationship with it. Relationship with the possessor of a deficiency is itself a deficiency and a setting. Hence, he says, "I have turned my face as one who is of pure faith to that which originated the heavens and the earth" [6:79]. The meaning of "that which" is an obscure allusion without relationship. If a speaker said, "What is the similitude for the concept of 'that which?'" one cannot conceive of an answer. Only the First, the Real, is incomparable with every relationship.

(15) This explains why, when a nomad said to the Messenger of God, "What is the lineage of God?"[2] there descended in answer, "Say: 'He is God, One, God the Everlasting Refuge, who has not begotten and has not been begotten, and equal to Him is not anyone'" [112:1–4]. The meaning is that God's "lineage" is too holy for and incomparable with any relationship. This is why, when Pharaoh said to Moses, "And what is the Lord of the worlds?" [26:23]—as if he were asking about His quiddity—Moses answered by informing Pharaoh of God's acts, since the acts are the most manifest of things in the questioner's eyes. Moses said, "The Lord of the heavens and the earth" [26:24]. Pharaoh said to those around him, "Did you not hear?" [26:25], like someone rebuking Moses for failing to answer the question of quiddity. Moses then said, "Your Lord and the Lord of your fathers, the ancients" [26:26]. So Pharaoh attributed madness to Moses, since he had asked for the similitude and the quiddity but he was answered with the acts. Thus he said, "Surely your Messenger who was sent to you is mad!" [26:27].

(16) Let us return to the example [promised to you above] and say:

(١٢) والسالك للطريق أولاً ينتهى إلى مادرجته درجة الكواكب فيتضح له إشراق نوره وينكشف له أن العالم الأسفل بأسره تحت سلطانه وتحت إشراق نوره؛ ويتضح له من جماله وعلو درجته مايبادر فيقول: «هذا ربى»

(١٣) ثم إذا اتضح له ما فوقه مما رتبته رتبة القمر، رأى دخول الأول في مغرب الهُوِىّ بالإضافة إلى ما فوقه فقال: «لا أحب الآفلين»

(١٤) وكذلك يترقى حتى ينتهى إلى ما مثاله الشمس فيراه أكبر وأعلى، فيراه قابلا للمثال بنوع مناسبة له معه. والمناسبة مع ذى النقص نقص وأفُول أيضاً. فنه يقول: «وجهت وجهى للذى فطر السموات والأرض حنيفاً». ومعنى «الذى» إشارة مبهمة لا مناسبة لها: إذ لو قال قائل ما مثال مفهوم «الذى» لم يتصور أن يجاب عنه. فالمتنزه عن كل مناسبة هو الأول الحق

(١٥) ولذلك لما قال بعض الأعراب لرسول الله صلى الله عليه وسلم: «ما نسب الإله؟» نزل في جوابه «قل هو الله أحد: الله الصمد: لم يلد ولم يولد» إلى آخرها. معناه أن التقدس والتنزه عن النسبة نسبته. ولذلك لما قال فرعون لموسى: «وما رب العالمين» كالطالب لماهيته، لم يجب إلا بتعريفه بأفعاله، إذ كانت الأفعال أظهر عند السائل، فقال: «رب السموات والأرض»، فقال فرعون لمن حوله «ألا تستمعون» كالمنكر عليه في عدوله في جوابه عن طلب الماهية، فقال موسى: «ربكم ورب آبائكم الأولين»، فنسبه فرعون إلى الجنون إذ كان مطلبه المثال والماهية؛ وهو يجيب عن الأفعال، فقال: «إن رسولكم الذى أرسل إليكم لمجنون»

(١٦) ولنرجع إلى الأنموذج فنقول.

(17) The science of dream interpretation makes known to you the way similitudes are struck, since dreams are a part of prophecy.[3] Do you not see that the sun in a dream is interpreted as the sultan? The reason is that the two share and are similar in a spiritual meaning, which is mastery over all and the effusion of effects upon everyone. The moon is interpreted as the vizier, since the absent sun effuses its light upon the world by means of the moon, just as the sultan effuses his lights upon the one who is absent from his presence by means of the vizier.

(18) When someone sees in his dream that he has a seal in his hand with which he seals the mouths of men and the private parts of women, its interpretation is that he is a muezzin who calls people to pray before dawn during the month of Ramadan.[4] When someone sees that he is pouring olive oil into an olive, the interpretation is that the slave girl below him is his mother, though he does not know it. A thorough examination of the various types of dream interpretation will increase your familiarity with this kind of thing, since it is not possible for me to occupy myself with listing them. Rather, I say:

(19) Among the high spiritual existents are those whose similitude is the sun, the moon, and the stars. So also there are among them things that have other similitudes, when attributes other than luminosity are in view. If there is among these existent things something that is fixed and unchanging, [something] that is great and not deemed small, and [something] from which the waters of the gnostic sciences and the jewels of unveilings gush into the riverbeds of human hearts, its similitude is "the mountain" [28:29].

(20) If there are existent things that receive these jewels and if some are more worthy than others, their similitude is the "riverbed." If these jewels, after becoming connected to human hearts, flow from heart to heart, these hearts are also "riverbeds." The initial source of the riverbed is the hearts of the prophets, then the *ʿulamāʾ*, then those who come after.

(١٧) علم «التعبير» يعرفك منهاج ضرب المثال؛ لأن الرؤيا جزء من النبوة. أما ترى أن الشمس في الرؤيا تعبيرها السلطان، لما بينهما من المشاركة والمماثلة في معنى روحانى—وهو الاستعلاء على الكافة مع فيضان الآثار على الجميع. والقمر تعبيره الوزير لإفاضة الشمس نورها بواسطة القمر على العالم عند غيبتها كما يفيض السلطان أنواره بواسطة الوزير على من يغيب عن حضرة السلطان.

(١٨) وأن من يرى أنه في يده خاتم يختم به أفواه الرجال وفروج النساء فتعبيره أنه مؤذن يؤذن قبل الصبح في رمضان. وأن من يرى أنه يصب الزيت في الزيتون فتعبيره أن تحته جارية هى أمه وهو لا يعرف. واستقصاء أبواب التعبير يزيدك أنساً بهذا الجنس، فلا يمكننى الاشتغال بعدّها: بل أقول:

(١٩) كما أن في الموجودات العالية الروحانية ما مثاله الشمس والقمر والكواكب، فكذلك فيها ما له أمثلة اخرى إذا اعتبرت منه أوصاف أخر سوى النورانية. فإن كان في تلك الموجودات ما هو ثابت لا يتغير وعظيم لا يستصغر، ومنه ينفجر إلى أودية القلوب البشرية مياه المعارف ونفائس المكاشفات فمثاله «الطّور»؛

(٢٠) وإن كان ثمّ موجودات تتلقى تلك النفائس بعضهم أولى من بعض فمثالها الوادى. وإن كانت تلك النفائس بعد اتصالها بالقلوب البشرية تجرى من قلب إلى قلب، فهذه القلوب أيضاً أودية. ومفتتح الوادى قلوب الأنبياء ثم العلماء ثم مَنْ بعدهم.

(21) If the later riverbeds are below the first and are fed by it, then it is appropriate that the first be the "blessed riverbed" [28:30], because of the abundance of its blessedness and the height of its degree.

(22) If the lowest riverbed takes from the last degree of the "blessed riverbed," then its feeding place is the "bank of the blessed riverbed" [28:30], not its bottom or its origin.

(23) If the spirit of the Prophet is a "light-giving lamp" [33:46] and is kindled by means of the divine revelation, as God said—"We have revealed to thee a Spirit of our bidding" [42:52]—then the similitude of that from which kindling takes place is "fire."

(24) If some of those who learn from the prophets do so through sheer imitation of what they hear, while others have a share of insight, the similitude of the portion of those who imitate is "a report" [28:29], while the similitude of the portion of the insightful is "a live coal" [28:29], "a burning brand" [20:10], and "a flame" [27:7], since the possessor of tasting shares with the prophets in some states. The similitude of this sharing is "warming oneself" [28:29], since only the person who has a fire can warm himself, not the person who hears a report about fire.

(25) If the first waystation of the prophets is to climb to the world that is too holy for the murkiness of sense perception and imagination, the similitude of this waystation is the "holy riverbed" [20:12].[5]

(26) If one is only able to walk in this holy riverbed by throwing off both this world and the next world and by turning one's face toward the One, the Real—because this world and the next world are two contraries and counterparts, and because they are accidents of the luminous human substance and can be thrown off at one time and put on at another—then the similitude of throwing off the two worlds when one consecrates oneself by turning one's face toward the *Ka*^{c}*aba* of holiness is "doffing the two sandals" [20:12].

(٢١) فإن كانت هذه الأودية دون الأول وعنها تغترف، فبالحرِىّ أن يكون الأول هو الوادى الأيمن لكثرة يمْنه وعلو درجته.

(٢٢) وإن كان الوادى الأدون يتلقى من آخر درجات الوادى الأيمن فمغترفه شاطىء الوادى الأيمن دون لجته ومبدئه.

(٢٣) وإن كان روح النبى سراجاً منيراً، وكان ذلك الروح مقتبساً بواسطة وحى كما قال: «أوحينا إليك روحاً من أمرنا» فما منه الاقتباس مثاله النار،

(٢٤) وإن كان المتلقنون من الأنبياء بعضهم على محض التقليد لما سمعه، وبعضهم على حظ من البصيرة، فمثال حظ المقلد الخبر، ومثال حظ المستبصر الجذوة والقبس والشهاب. فإن صاحب الذوق مشارك للنبى في بعض الأحوال. ومثال تلك المشاركة الاصطلاء. وإنما يصطلى بالنار من معه النار، لامن يسمع خبرها.

(٢٥) وإن كان أول منزل الأنبياء الترقي إلى العالم المقدس عن كدورة الحس والخيال، فمثال ذلك المنزل الوادى المقدس.

(٢٦) وإن كان لا يمكن وطء ذلك الوادى المقدس إلا باطّراح الكونين—أعنى الدنيا والآخرة—والتوجه إلى الواحد الحق، ولأن الدنيا والآخرة متقابلتان متحاذيتان وهما عارضان للجوهر النورانى البشرى يمكن اطراحهما مرة والتلبس بهما أخرى، فمثال اطّراحهما عند الإحرام للتوجه إلى كعبة القدس خلع النعلين.

(27) But let us climb once more to the presence of lordship. We say: If there is, in this presence, something through which the differentiated sciences are engraved upon substances receptive to it, the similitude of this thing is “the pen” [of God] [68:1, 96:4].

(28) If some of these receptive substances are prior in receiving, so that they transfer these sciences to others, their similitude is “the preserved tablet” [85:22] and “the unrolled parchment” [of God] [52:3].

(29) If there is something above the engraver of the sciences that controls it, then its similitude is “the hand” [of God] [23:88].

(30) If this presence—which comprises the hand, the tablet, the pen, and the book—has a regular hierarchy, then the similitude of this hierarchy is “the form.”

(31) And if the human form is found to have a hierarchy that takes this shape, then the human form is “in the form of the All-Merciful.” There is a difference between saying “in the form of the All-Merciful” and “in the form of God,” because the divine mercy is that to which the Divine Presence gives form through the [human] form.[6]

(32) God showed beneficence to Adam. He gave him an abridged form that brings together every sort of thing found in the cosmos. It is as if Adam is everything in the cosmos, or an abridged transcription of the world. The form of Adam—I mean this form—is written in God’s handwriting. It is a divine handwriting that is not written with letters, since God’s handwriting is incomparable with writing and letters, just as His speech is incomparable with sounds and letters, His pen with wood and reed, and His hand with flesh and bone.

(33) If it were not for this mercy, human beings would not be capable of knowing their Lord, since one knows one’s Lord only by knowing oneself.[7] Since this [knowing] is one of the effects of the divine mercy, Adam came to be in the form of the All-Merciful and not in the form

(٢٧) بل نترقي إلى حضرة الربوبية مرة أخرى ونقول: إن كان في تلك الحضرة شيء بواسطته تنتقش العلوم المفصّلة في الجواهر القابلة لها فمثاله «القلم».

(٢٨) وإن كان في تلك الجواهر القابلة ما بعضها سابق إلى التلق، ومنها تنتقل إلى غيرها، فمثالها «اللوح المحفوظ» و «الرق المنشور».

(٢٩) وإن كان فوق الناقش للعلوم شيء هو مسخر فمثاله «اليد».

(٣٠) وإن كان لهذه الحضرة المشتملة على اليد واللوح والقلم والكتاب ترتيب منظوم فمثاله «الصورة».

(٣١) وإن كان يوجد للصورة الإنسية نوع ترتيب على هذه الشاكلة، فهى على صورة الرحمن. وفرق بين أن يقال «على صورة الرحمن» وبين أن يقال «على صورة الله» لأن الرحمة الإلهية هى التى صورتها الحضرة الإلهية بهذه الصورة.

(٣٢) ثم أنعم على آدم فأعطاه صورة مختصرة جامعة لجميع أصناف ما في العالم حتى كأنه كل ما في العالم أو هو نسخة من العالم مختصرة. وصورة آدم — أعنى هذه الصورة — مكتوبة بخط الله. فهو الخط الإلهى الذى ليس برقم حروف، إذ تنزه خطه عن أن يكون رقماً وحروفاً كما تنزه كلامه (عن) أن يكون صوتاً وحرفاً، وقلمه عن أن يكون خشباً وقصباً، ويده عن أن تكون لحماً وعظماً.

(٣٣) ولولا هذه الرحمة لعجز الآدمى عن معرفة ربه: إذ لا يعرف ربه إلا من عرف نفسه. فلما كان هذا من آثار الرحمة صار على صورة الرحمن لا على

of God. For the presence of divinity is different from the presence of mercy, the presence of kingship, and the presence of lordship. That is why God commanded taking refuge with all these presences, for He said, "Say: 'I take refuge with the Lord of men, the King of men, the God of men'" [114:1–3]. If it were not for this meaning, it would have been appropriate for Him to say, "in His own form." But the words mentioned in the sound *ḥadīth* are "upon the form of the All-Merciful."[8]

(34) Distinguishing the presence of kingship from the presence of divinity and lordship would call for a long explanation, so let us pass it by. And let this much of the example be sufficient for you, since this discussion is an ocean without shore. If you find yourself put off by these similitudes, then make your heart intimate with His words: "He sends down out of heaven water and the riverbeds flow each in its measure" [13:17], and with the fact that the Qurʾānic commentaries say that water is knowledge and the Qurʾān, while the riverbeds are hearts.

Conclusion and apology

(35) Do not suppose from this example and this way of striking similitudes that I permit the abolishing of outward meanings and that I believe in their nullification, so that I would say, for example, that Moses did not have two sandals, and that he did not hear God address him with the words, "Doff your two sandals!" [20:12]. God forbid! Nullifying the outward meanings is the view of the Bāṭinites, who have one blind eye and look only at one of the two worlds, not recognizing the parallel between the two or understanding its significance. In the same way, nullifying the inner mysteries is the path of the literalists. Hence, those who look only at the outward are literalists, those who look only at the inward are Bāṭinites, and those who bring the two together are perfect. This is why the Prophet said, "The Qurʾān has an outward, an inward, a limit, and a place to which one ascends." Perhaps this saying is transmitted from ʿAlī and stops with him.[9]

صورة الله: فإن حضرة الإلهية غير حضرة الرحمة وغير حضرة الملك وغير حضرة الربوبية. ولذلك أمر بالعياذ بجميع هذه الحضرات فقال: «قل أعوذ برب الناس، ملك الناس، إله الناس» ولولا هذا المعنى لكان ينبغي أن يقول «على صورته» واللفظ الوارد في (الحديث) الصحيح (على صورة الرحمن).

(٣٤) ولأن تمييز حضرة الملك عن الإلهية والربوبية يستدعى شرحاً طويلاً، فلنتجاوزه، ويكفيك من الأنموذج هذا القدر، فإن هذا بحر لا ساحل له. فإن وجدت في نفسك نفوراً عن هذه الأمثال فآنِسْ قلبك بقوله تعالى: «أنزل من السماء ماء فسالت أودية بقدرها» الآية، وأنه كيف ورد في التفسير أن الماء هو المعرفة والقرآن، والأودية القلوب.

خاتمة واعتذار

(٣٥) لا تظنن من هذا الأنموذج وطريق ضرب المثال رخصة مني في رفع الظواهر واعتقاداً في إبطالها حتى أقول مثلاً لم يكن مع موسى نعلان، ولم يسمع الخطاب بقوله «اخلع نعليك». حاش لله! فإن إبطال الظواهر رأى الباطنية الذين نظروا بالعين العوراء إلى أحد العالمين ولم يعرفوا الموازنة بين العالمين، ولم يفهموا وجهه. كما أن إبطال الأسرار مذهب الحشوية. فالذى يجرد الظاهر حشوى، والذى يجرد الباطن باطنى. والذى يجمع بينهما كامل. ولذلك قال عليه السلام: «للقرآن ظاهر وباطن وحدٌ ومطلع» وربما نقل هذا عن علىّ موقوفاً عليه.

(36) What I say is this: By the command to doff the two sandals, Moses understood throwing off the two engendered worlds. Hence, he obeyed the command outwardly by doffing the sandals and inwardly by throwing off the two worlds. This is "the crossing over"—that is, the crossing from one thing to another and from the outward to the mystery.

(37) There is a difference between people: One person hears the words of God's Messenger: "The angels do not enter a house in which there is a dog,"[10] and [yet] brings a dog into his house. He says, "The outward sense is not meant; on the contrary, what is meant is removing the dog of anger from the house of the heart, because it prevents the entrance of knowledge, which derives from the lights of angels, since anger is the ghoul of the rational faculty." Another person obeys the outward sense of the command. Then he says, "The dog is not a dog because of its form, but because of its meaning, which is predatoriness and ferocity. If it is incumbent to preserve the house, which is the resting place of the person and body, from the dog's form, then it is even more incumbent to preserve the house of the heart—the resting place of the specific true substance [of humanity]—from the doglike evil.[11] Thereby I bring together the outward and the mystery."

(38) Such a person is perfect. It is he [who is] meant by their words: "When someone is perfect, the light of his knowledge does not extinguish the light of his piety." Hence, you see that the perfect one does not allow himself to leave aside a single prescription of the *sharīʿa,* even though he has perfect insight.

(39) This is an error that makes some of the travelers slip into license and roll up the carpet of the outward statutes. It may even happen that one of them will abandon the prescribed ritual prayers and suppose that he is in perpetual prayer in his innermost consciousness. This is the same as the error of those stupid people who give themselves license by seizing on nonsensical sayings like the words of one of them, "God does not need our works," and the words of another, "The inner self is full of loathsome things and cannot be purified." They do not desire to uproot anger and appetite, since they suppose that they are commanded

(٣٦) بل أقول فهم موسى من الأمر بخلع النعلين اطّراح الكونين فامتثل الأمر ظاهراً بخلع نعليه، وباطناً باطراح العالمين. وهذا هو «الاعتبار» أى العبور من الشيء إلى غيره، ومن الظاهر إلى السر.

(٣٧) وفرق بين من يسمع قول رسول الله صلى الله عليه وسلم: «لا يدخل الملائكة بيتاً فيه كلب» فيقتنى الكلب في البيت ويقول ليس الظاهر مراداً، بل المراد تخلية بيت القلب عن كلب الغضب لأنه يمنع المعرفة التى هى من أنوار الملائكة: إذ الغضب غول العقل، وبين من يمتثل الأمر في الظاهر ثم يقول: الكلب ليس كلباً لصورته بل لمعناه--وهو السبعية والضراوة--وإذا كان حفظ البيت الذى هو مقر الشخص والبدن واجباً عن صورة الكلب، فبأن يجب حفظ بيت القلب--وهو مقر الجوهر الحقيق الخاص--عن شر الكلبية أولى. فأنا أجمع بين الظاهر والسر جميعاً،

(٣٨) فهذا هو الكامل: وهو المعنىّ بقولهم «الكامل من لا يطفىء نور معرفته نور ورعه». ولذلك ترى الكامل لا تسمح نفسه بترك حد من حدود الشرع مع كمال البصيرة.

(٣٩) وهذه مَغْلطة منها وقع بعض السالكين إلى الإباحة وطى بساط الأحكام ظاهراً، حتى أنه ربما ترك أحدهم الصلاة وزعم أنه دائماً في الصلاة بسره. وهذا سوى مغلطة الحمق من الإباحية الذين مأخذهم ترّهات كقول بعضهم «إن الله غنى عن عملنا»، وقول بعضهم إن الباطن مشحون بالخبائث ليس يمكن تزكيته، ولا يطمع في استئصال الغضب والشهوة لظنه أنه مأمور

to uproot them. This is all stupidity. All that we mentioned is the slip of the high-minded and the stumble of the traveler—he whom Satan envies and pulls down with the cord of delusion.[12]

(40) Let me return to the discussion of the two sandals. I say: The outward doffing of the sandals calls attention to the abandonment of the two engendered worlds. Hence, the similitude in the outward aspect is true, and its giving rise to the inward mystery is a reality.

(41) Those who are worthy of having their attention called through this similitude have reached the degree of the "glass," in the sense in which the glass will be discussed. Imagination, which provides the clay from which the similitude is taken, is solid and dense. It veils the mysteries and comes between you and the lights. But when the imagination is purified so that it becomes like clear glass, then it does not obstruct the lights; rather, it becomes a pointer toward the lights; or, rather, it preserves the lights from being extinguished by violent winds. The story of the "glass" will be told shortly.

(42) Know that the low, dense, imaginal world became for the prophets a glass, a niche for lights, a purifier of the mysteries, and a ladder to the highest world. Through this it comes to be known that the outward similitude is true and behind it is a mystery. Deal in the same way with the similitudes of the "mountain," the "fire," and so on.

A fine point

(43) The Messenger said, "I saw ʿAbd al-Raḥmān ibn ʿAwf entering the Garden crawling."[13] Do not suppose that he did not witness it with his eyesight in just this manner. On the contrary, he saw it in wakefulness, just as a sleeping person would see it in a dream, even if, for example, ʿAbd al-Raḥmān himself was asleep in his house. Sleep has an effect on witnessings such as these because the ruling authority of the senses forces the person to turn away from the inward divine light, since the senses keep him occupied and attract him toward the world of sense perception, turning his face away from the world of the unseen and the dominion.

باستئصالهما: وهذه حماقات. فأما ما ذكرناه فهو كبوة جواد وهفوة سالك حسده الشيطان فدلأه بحبْل الغرور.

(٤٠) وأرجع إلى حديث النعلين فأقول: ظاهر خلع النعلين منبه على ترك الكونين. فالمثال في الظاهر حق وأداؤة إلى السر الباطن حقيقة

(٤١) وأهل هذا التنبيه هم الذين بلغوا درجة الزجاجة كما سيأتى معنى الزجاجة؛ لأن الخيال الذى من طينته يتخذ المثال صلب كثيف يحجب الأسرار ويحول بينك وبين الأنوار؛ ولكن إذا صفا حتى صار كالزجاج الصافي غير حائل عن الأنوار، بل صار مع ذلك مؤدياً للأنوار، بل صار مع ذلك حافظاً للأنوار عن الانطفاء بعواصف الرياح. وستأتيك قصة الزجاجة.

(٤٢) فاعلم أن العالم الكثيف الخيالى السفلى صار في حق الأنبياء زجاجة ومشكاة للأنوار ومصفاء للأسرار، ومرقاة إلى العالم الأعلى. وبهذا يعرف أن المثال الظاهر حق ووراءه سر. وقس على هذا «الطّور» و «النار» وغيرهما.

دقيقة

(٤٣) إذا قال الرسول عليه السلام: «رأيت عبد الرحمن بن عوف يدخل الجنة حَبْوًا» فلا تظنن أنه لم يشاهده بالبصر كذلك، بل رآه في يقظته كما يراه النائم في نومه؛ وإن كان عبد الرحمن مثلاً نائماً في بيته بشخصه، فإن النوم إنما أثر في أمثال هذه المشاهدات لقهره سلطان الحواس عن النور الباطن الإلهى، فإن الحواس شاغلة له وجاذبة إياه إلى عالم الحس، وصارفة وجْهَه عن عالم الغيب والملكوت.

(44) But it may happen that some of the prophetic lights rise up and take control. Then the senses do not draw him to their world and do not keep him occupied. He witnesses in wakefulness what someone else would witness in a dream. But when he dwells in the utmost limit of perfection, his perception is not confined simply to the seen form. Rather, he crosses from it to the mystery. Then it is unveiled to him that faith attracts to a world that is called "the Garden," while riches and wealth attract to the present life, which is the lower world. If that which attracts to the business of this world is stronger or it resists the other attraction, then the person is blocked from journeying to the Garden. If the attraction of faith is stronger, the other attraction will result in difficulty and slowness in his journey. Hence, the similitude for this journey from the visible world is "crawling." In this way, the lights of the mysteries are disclosed to the viewer from behind the pieces of glass that are the imagination.

(45) The Messenger did not limit his judgment to ᶜAbd al-Raḥmān alone, even though his vision was restricted to him. Rather, through him he made a judgment concerning everyone whose insight is strengthened, whose faith is firm, and whose wealth becomes so abundant that it competes with faith but cannot overcome it, because the strength of faith is greater.

(46) This lets you know how the prophets see forms and how they witness the meanings behind the forms. In most cases, the meaning is prior to the inward witnessing. Then the meaning radiates from the witnessing upon the imaginal spirit, whereupon the imagination becomes imprinted with a form that parallels the meaning and resembles it. This type of revelation in wakefulness needs interpretation, just as in dreams it needs dream interpretation. That which occurs in dreams is related to the prophetic characteristics, just as [the number] one is related to forty-six,[14] while that which occurs in wakefulness is more closely related than this. I suppose that its relationship is that of one to three, since the branches of the prophetic characteristics that have been unveiled to us are confined to three, and this is one of the three kinds.[15]

(٤٤) وبعض الأنوار النبوية قد يستعلى ويستولى بحيث لا تستجره الحواس إلى عالمها ولا تشغله، فيشاهد في اليقظة ما يشاهد غيره في المنام. ولكنه إذا كان في غاية الكمال لم يقتصر إدراكه على محض الصورة المبصرة، بل عَبر منها إلى السر فانكشف له أن الإيمان جاذب إلى العالم الذى يعبر عنه بالجنة؛ والغنى والثروة جاذب إلى الحياة الحاضرة وهى العالم الأسفل. فإن كان الجاذب إلى أشغال الدنيا أقوى أو مقاوماً للجاذب الآخر صُدّعن المسير إلى الجنة. وإن كان جاذب الايمان أقوى أورث عسراً وبطئاً في سيره؛ فيكون مثاله من عالم الشهادة «الحبْو». فكذلك تتجلى له أنوار الأسرار من وراء زجاجات الخيال

(٤٥) ولذلك لا يقتصر في حكمه على عبد الرحمن وإن كان إبصاره مقصوراً عليه، بل يحكم به على كل من قويت بصيرته واستحكم إيمانه، وكثرت ثروته كثرة تزاحم الايمان لكن لا تقاومه لرجحان قوة الإيمان.

(٤٦) فهذا يعرّفك كيفية إبصار الأنبياء الصور وكيفية مشاهدتهم المعانى من وراء الصور. والأغلب أن يكون المعنى سابقاً إلى المشاهدة الباطنة ثم يشرق منها على الروح الخيالى فينطبع الخيال بصورة موازنة للمعنى محاكية له. وهذا النمط من الوحى في اليقظة يفتقر إلى التأويل، كما أنه في النوم يفتقر إلى التعبير. والواقع منه في النوم نسبته إلى الخواص النبوية نسبة الواحد إلى ستة وأربعين. والواقع في اليقظة نسبته أعظم من ذلك. وأظن أن نسبته إليه نسبة الواحد إلى الثلاثة. فإن [الذى] انكشف لنا من الخواص النبوية ينحصر شعبها في ثلاثة أجناس، وهذا واحد من تلك الأجناس الثلاثة.

The second pole

Clarifying the levels of the luminous human spirits;
for, through knowing them, you will
come to know the similitudes of the Qurʾān

(47) The first of the luminous human spirits is the sensible spirit. It is the one that receives what the five senses bring. It seems to be the root and first appearance of the animal spirit, since through it the animal becomes an animal. It is found in the suckling child.

(48) The second is the imaginal spirit. This spirit seeks to fix what the senses bring in, remembering it as something stored within itself, in order to present it to the rational spirit above it when there is need for it. This spirit is not found in the suckling child at the beginning of its growth. That is why an infant tries eagerly to take something, but when it is absent from him he forgets about it and his soul does not make him yearn for it. When he becomes a little older, he reaches a point where he cries and demands a thing even when it is hidden from him, because its form remains preserved in his imagination. This spirit is found in some animals and not in others. It is not found in the moth that pounces upon fire, aspiring for the fire because of its passionate love for the brightness of day. It supposes that the lamp is a window opened onto a place of brightness, so it throws itself upon it and is harmed by it. But when it passes by the fire and reaches darkness, it returns to the fire time after time. If it had a remembering spirit that fixed the pain conveyed to it by its senses, it would not return to it after having been harmed a single time. Thus, when a dog is beaten once with a stick, it flees when it sees the stick from afar.

(49) The third is the rational spirit through which you perceive meanings outside of the senses and imagination. This spirit is the specific human substance. It is not found in beasts or in children. The

القطب الثانى

فى بيان مراتب الأرواح البشرية النورانية.

إذ بمعرفتها تعرف أمثلة القرآن.

(٤٧) فالأول منها الروح الحساس، وهو الذى يتلقى ما تورده الحواس الخمس، وكأنه أصل الروح الحيوانى وأوله، إذ به يصير الحيوان حيواناً. وهو موجود للصبى الرضيع.

(٤٨) الثانى الروح الخيالى، وهو الذى يستثبت ما أورده الحواس ويحفظه مخزوناً عنده ليعرضه على الروح العقلى الذى فوقه عند الحاجة إليه. وهذا لا يوجد للصبى الرضيع في بداية نشوئه: ولذلك يولع بالشىء ليأخذه، فإذا غاب عنه ينساه ولاتنازعه نفسه إليه إلى أن يكبر قليلاً فيصير بحيث إذا غُيِّب عنه بكى وطلب [ذلك] لبقاء صورته محفوظة في خياله. وهذا قد يوجد لبعض الحيوانات دون بعض، ولا يوجد للفراش المتهافت على النار لأنه يقصد النار لشغفه بضياء النهار: فيظن أن السراج كوة مفتوحة إلى موضع الضياء فيلقى نفسه عليه فيتأذى به. لكنه إذا جاوزه وحصل في الظلمة عاوده مرة بعد مرة. ولو كان له الروح الحافظ المستثبت لما أداه الحس إليه من الألم لما عاوده بعد أن تضرر مرة به. فالكلب إذا ضرب مرة بخشبة، فإذا رأى الخشبة بعد ذلك من بعد هرب.

(٤٩) الثالث الروح العقلى الذى به تدرك المعانى الخارجة عن الحس والخيال، وهو الجوهر الإنسى الخاص، ولا يوجد لا للبهائم ولا للصبيان.

objects of its perception are universal self-evident knowledge, just as we mentioned when we showed the superiority of the light of the rational faculty over the light of the eye.

(50) The fourth level is the reflective spirit. It takes pure rational knowledge and brings about combinations and pairings, deducing therefrom noble knowledge. Then, for example, when it derives two conclusions, it combines the two anew and derives another conclusion. It never ceases increasing in this manner *ad infinitum*.

(51) The fifth is the holy prophetic spirit that is singled out for the prophets and some of the friends of God. Within it are disclosed flashes of the unseen, the properties of the next world, and some of the knowledge of the dominion of the heavens and the earth, or, rather, some of the lordly knowledge that the rational and reflective spirits cannot reach. There is an allusion to this in God's words, "Even so We have revealed to thee a Spirit of Our command. Thou knewest not what the Book was, nor faith; but We made it a light, whereby We guide whom We will of Our servants" [42:52]. For it is not unlikely—O you who cling to the world of the rational faculty—that there is another stage beyond the rational faculty within which there becomes manifest that which does not become manifest to the rational faculty. In the same way, it is not unlikely that the rational faculty is a stage that lies beyond discrimination and sensation, within which marvels and wonders are unveiled that sensation and discrimination cannot reach.[16] Do not think that utmost perfection stops at your own self.

(52) If you desire a similitude of this taken from all the characteristics we witness in some people, then consider how taste in poetry, which is a kind of sensation and perception, is singled out for a single group of men. Some people are so deprived of this taste that, for them, harmonious melodies cannot be distinguished from the disharmonious. Consider also how the strength of taste within some people is so great that they derive from it music, songs, stringed instruments, and many types of musical modes which produce sadness, delight, sleep, laughter,

ومدركاته المعارف الضرورية الكلية كما ذكرناه عند ترجيح نور العقل على نور العين.

(٥٠) الرابع الروح الفكرى، وهو الذى يأخذ العلوم العقلية المحضة فيوقع بينها تأليفات وازدواجات ويستنتج منها معارف شريفة. ثم إذا استفاد نتيجتين مثلاً، ألف بينهما مرة أخرى واستفاد نتيجة أخرى. ولا يزال يتزايد كذلك إلى غير نهاية.

(٥١) الخامس الروح القدسى النبوى الذى يختص به الأنبياء وبعض الأولياء، وفيه تتجلى لوائح الغيب وأحكام الآخرة وجملة من معارف ملكوت السموات والأرض، بل من المعارف الربانية التى يقصر دونها الروح العقلى والفكرى. وإليه الإشارة بقوله تعالى: «وكذلك أوحينا إليك روحاً من أمرنا ما كنت تدرى ما الكتاب ولا الايمان، ولكن جعلناه نوراً نهدى به» الآية. فلا يبعد أيها العاكف في عالم العقل أن يكون وراء العقل طور آخر يظهر فيه ما لا يظهر في العقل، كما لا يبعد كون العقل طوراً وراء التميز والإحساس تنكشف فيه غرائب وعجائب يقصر عنها الإحساس والتميز. ولا تجعل أقصى الكمال وقفاً على نفسك.

(٥٢) وإن أردت مثالاً مما نشاهده من جملة خواص بعض البشر فانظر إلى ذوق الشعر كيف يختص به قوم من الناس وهو نوع إحساس وإدراك، ويحرم عنه بعضهم حتى لا تتميز عندهم الألحان الموزونة من المنزحفة. وانظر كيف عظمت قوة الذوق في طائفة حتى استخرجوا بها الموسيقى والأغانى والأوتار وصنوف الدستانات التى منها المحزن ومنها المطرب ومنها المنوم ومنها المضحك

madness, slaying, and loss of consciousness. These effects are only strong in one who possesses the root of this taste. As for one devoid of the characteristic of taste, he also hears the sounds, but these effects are weak within him. He wonders at one who possesses ecstasy and loses consciousness. If all the rational thinkers who are masters of taste came together to make him understand the meaning of taste, they would not be able to do so. This is a similitude concerning a lowly situation, but it is near to your understanding.

(53) Use this similitude to understand the specific prophetic taste and strive to become one of those people who taste something of that spirit, for the friends of God have an ample portion of it. If you are not able to do this, then strive, through the analogies we mentioned and through the attention-calling remarks we gave as symbols, to become one of those people who have knowledge of this. If you are not able to do that, then the least you can do is [to] be one of those people who have faith in it. "God will raise up in degrees those of you who have faith and have been given knowledge" [58:11]. Knowledge is above faith, and tasting is above knowledge; [this] because tasting is a finding, but knowing is a drawing of analogies, and having faith is a mere acceptance through imitation. Therefore, have a good opinion of the people of finding and the people of gnosis.

(54) Once you have recognized these five spirits, know that, taken together, they are lights, because they make many types of existent things manifest—the sensory and imaginal among them. Even though the beasts share in certain kinds of spirit, the human being has another kind, nobler and higher. Humans were created for a more sublime and loftier objective. As for the animals, spirits were created for them only to be their instrument in the search for nourishment while they are subject to human beings. The spirits were created for human beings only to be their net in the lower world—a net with which they can catch the principles of the noble religious sciences. When a human being perceives a particular individual with the senses, the rational faculty acquires from it a general, unlimited meaning, just as we mentioned concerning the similitude of ʿAbd al-Raḥmān ibn ʿAwf crawling. Since you now know these five spirits, let us return to the presentation of the similitudes.

ومنها المجنن ومنها القاتل، ومنها الموجب للغشى. وإنما تقوى هذه الآثار فيمن له أصل الذوق. وأما العاطل عن خاصية الذوق فيشارك في سماع الصوت وتضعف فيه هذه الآثار، وهو يتعجب من صاحب الوجد والغش. ولو اجتمع العقلاء كلهم من أرباب الذوق على تفهيمه معنى الذوق لم يقدروا عليه. فهذا مثال في أمر خسيس لكنه قريب إلى فهمك.

(٥٣) فقسْ به الذوق الخاص النبوى واجتهد أن تصير من أهل الذوق بشيء من ذلك الروح: فإن للأولياء منه حظاً وافراً. فإن لم تقدر فاجتهد أن تصير بالأقيسة التى ذكرناها والتنبيهات التى رمزنا إليها من أهل العلم بها. فإن لم تقدر فلا أقل من أن تكون من أهل الإيمان بها: و «يرفع الله الذين آمنوا منكم والذين أوتوا العلم درجات». والعلم فوق الإيمان، والذوق فوق العلم. فالذوق وجدان والعلم قياس. والإيمان قبول مجرد بالتقليد. وحسْن الظن بأهل الوجدان أو بأهل العرفان.

(٥٤) فإذا عرفت هذه الأرواح الخمسة فاعلم أنها بجملتها أنوار لأنها تظهر أصناف الموجودات، والحسى والخيالى منها، وإن كان يشارك البهائم في جنسها، لكن الذى للإنسان منه نمط آخر أشرف وأعلى؛ وخلق الإنسان لأجل غرض أجلّ وأسمى. أما الحيوانات فلم يخلق ذلك لها إلا ليكون آلتها في طلب غذائها في تسخيرها للآدمى. وإنما خلق للآدمى ليكون شبكة له يقتنص بها من العالم الأسفل مبادئ المعارف الدينية الشريفة. إذ الإنسان إذا أدرك بالحس شخصاً معيناً اقتبس عقله منه معنى عاماً مطلقاً كما ذكرنا في مثال حبْو عبد الرحمن بن عوف. وإذا عرفت هذه الأرواح الخمسة فلنرجع إلى عرض الأمثلة.

A clarification of the similitudes of this verse

(55) Know that drawing a parallel between these five spirits and the niche, the glass, the lamp, the tree, and the olive can be a long discussion. But I will be brief and confine it to calling attention to the path of drawing parallels. I say:

(56) As for the sensible spirit, when you consider its specific characteristic, you find that its lights come out of numerous holes, like the two eyes, the two ears, the two nostrils, and so forth. Hence, the most suitable similitude for this spirit in the visible world is the niche.

(57) As for the imaginal spirit, we find that it has three characteristics: First is that it derives from the clay of the dense low world, because the imaginalized thing possesses measure [and] shape, [has] specified and confined directions, and is near or far relative to the one who does the imagining. A characteristic of a dense thing that is described by the attributes of bodies is that it veils the pure rational lights, which are incomparable with being described in terms of directions, measures, nearness, and farness.

(58) The second characteristic is that when this dense imagination is purified, refined, polished, and organized, it becomes parallel to the rational meanings and points toward their lights. It does not obstruct the light that radiates from the meanings.

(59) The third characteristic is that, at the beginning, imagination is much needed, because through it one can organize rational knowledge so that knowledge will not be agitated, shaken up, and scattered with a scattering that eliminates the organization. What a wonderful help are the imaginal similitudes for rational knowledge!

(60) We find these three characteristics in relation to the seen lights of the visible world only in glass. Originally, glass is a dense substance, but once it is purified and made clear, it does not veil the light

بيان أمثلة هذه الآية

(٥٥) اعلم أن القول في موازنة هذه الأرواح الخمسة للمشكاة والزجاجة والمصباح والشجرة والزيت يمكن تطويله، لكنى أو جزه وأقتصر على التنبيه على طريقه فأقول:

(٥٦) أما الروح الحساس فإذا نظرت إلى خاصيته وجدت أنواره خارجة من ثُقَب عدة كالعينين والأذنين والمنخرين وغيرها. وأوفق مثال له من عالم الشهادة المشكاة.

(٥٧) وأما الروح الخيالى فنجد له خواص ثلاثاً: إحداها: أنه من طينة العالم السفلى الكثيف: لأن الشيء المتخيل ذو مقدار وشكل وجهات محصورة مخصوصة. وهو على نسبة من المتخيل من قرب أو بعد. ومن شأن الكثيف الموصوف بأوصاف الأجسام أن يحجب عن الأنوار العقلية المحضة التى تتنزه عن الوصف بالجهات والمقادير والقرب والبعد.

(٥٨) الثانية: أن هذا الخيال الكثيف إذا صفيَ ودقق وهذّب وضبط صار موازياً للمعانى العقلية ومؤدياً لأنوارها، غير حائل عن إشراق نورها منها

(٥٩) الثالث: أن الخيال في بداية الأمر محتاج إليه جداً ليضبط به المعارف العقلية فلا تضطرب ولا تتزلزل ولا تنتشر انتشاراً يخرج عن الضبط. فنعم المعين المثالات الخيالية للمعارف العقلية.

(٦٠) وهذه الخواص الثلاث لا نجدها في عالم الشهادة بالإضافة إلى الأنوار المبصرة إلا للزجاجة: فإنها في الأصل من جوهر كثيف لكن صُفيَ ورقق حتى

of the lamp. Rather, it conveys the light in a proper manner. Furthermore, it protects the light from being extinguished by violent winds and rough movements. Glass, therefore, is the first similitude for the imaginal spirit.

(61) As for the third spirit—the rational spirit through which perception of noble, divine knowledge takes place—the manner of using the lamp as a similitude for it is not hidden from you. You came to know this in the earlier clarification of the fact that the prophets are light-giving lamps.[17]

(62) As for the fourth spirit—the reflective spirit—one of its specific characteristics is that it begins with a single root and then branches off from it into two branches. Then from each branch grow two branches, and so on until the branches of rational divisions become many. Then, at last, it reaches conclusions that are its fruits. These fruits then go back and become seeds for similar fruits, because some of them can fertilize others so that they continue to bear fruits beyond them. This is similar to what we mentioned in the book *The Just Balance*.[18] Hence, it is most appropriate that in this world the similitude of the reflective spirit be the tree.

(63) Since the fruits of the reflective spirit are a matter within which the lights of knowledge may be augmented, fixed, and given subsistence, it is appropriate that the likeness that is used not be the quince, apple, pomegranate, or other [kinds of] trees. But, among all the trees, the olive tree specifically is used, because the quintessence of its fruit is olive oil, which is the matter for lamps. Out of all oils, olive oil is singled out for the specific characteristic of having a great deal of radiance with little smoke.

(64) If cattle and trees that have many offspring and much fruit are called "blessed," then it is even more worthy to call that tree whose fruit does not end at a defined limit a "blessed tree" [24:35].

(65) If the branches of pure rational thoughts cannot be ascribed to directions [or to] nearness and farness, then it is appropriate that the tree be "neither of the East nor the West" [24:35].

لا يحجب نور المصباح بل يؤديه على وجهه، ثم يحفظه عن الانطفاء بالرياح العاصفة والحركات العنيفة. فهى أول مثال له.

(٦١) وأما الثالث وهو الروح العقلى الذى به إدراك المعارف الشريفة الإلهية فلا يخفى عليك وجه تمثيله بالمصباح. وقد عرفت هذا فيما سبق من بيان كون الأنبياء سُرُجاً منيرة

(٦٢) وأما الرابع وهو الروح الفكرى فمن خاصيته أنه يبتدئ من أصل واحد ثم تتشعب منه شعبتان، ثم من كل شعبة شعبتان وهكذا إلى أن تكثر الشعب بالتقسيمات العقلية، ثم يفضى بالآخرة إلى نتائج هى ثمراتها. ثم تلك الثمرات تعود فتصير بذوراً لأمثالها: إذ يمكن أيضاً تلقيح بعضها بالبعض حتى يتمادى إلى ثمرات وراءها كما ذكرناه في كتاب القسطاس المستقيم، فبالحرِىّ أن يكون مثاله من هذا العالم السجرِة.

(٦٣) وإذ كانت ثمراته مادة لتضاعف أنوار المعارف وثباتها وبقائها فبالحرِىّ ألاتمثل بشجرة السفرجل والتفاح والرمان وغيرها، بل من جملة سائر الأشجار بالزيتونة خاصة: لأن لب ثمرها هو الزيت الذى هو مادة المصابيح، ويختص من سائر الأدهان بخاصية زيادة الإشراق مع قلة الدخان.

(٦٤) وإذا كانت الماشية التى يكثر نسلها والشجرة التى تكثر ثمرتها تسمى مباركة، فالتى لا يتناهى ثمرتها إلى حد محدود أوْلى أن تسمى شجرة مباركة.

(٦٥) وإذا كانت شعب الأفكار العقلية المحضة خارجة عن قبول الإضافة إلى الجهات والقرب والبعد، فبالحرِىّ أن تكون لا شرقية ولا غربية.

(66) The fifth spirit is the holy prophetic spirit ascribed to the friends of God when it is in the utmost degree of purity and nobility.

(67) The reflective spirit is divided into [two kinds:] a sort that needs instruction, awakening, and help from the outside so that it may continue partaking of many types of knowledge; and another sort that has such intense purity that it is, as it were, awakened by itself without help from the outside. It is most appropriate that the one that is pure and has reached full preparedness be referred to by the words, "Its oil would well-nigh but shine, even if no fire touched it" [24:35], since among the friends of God are those whose light would all but shine so that they could all but dispense with the help of the prophets. And among the prophets are those who could all but dispense with the help of the angels. This similitude is suitable for this kind.

(68) When these lights are ranked in levels, one on top of the other, then the sensory spirit is the first. It is like the preparation and introduction to the imaginal spirit, since the imaginal cannot be conceived of as being placed in its situation except after the sensory. The reflective and rational spirits come after these two. Hence, it is most appropriate that the glass be like the locus for the lamp and the niche like the locus for the glass. Hence, the lamp is in a glass and the glass is in a niche. Since all of them are lights, one above the other, it is appropriate that they be "light upon light" [24:35].

A conclusion

(69) This similitude becomes clear only to the hearts of those who have faith or to the hearts of the prophets and the friends of God, not to the hearts of the unbelievers. After all, by "guidance" is meant light. That which is kept away from the path of guidance is falsehood and darkness—or, rather, it is more intense than darkness, because darkness does not guide to falsehood any more than it guides to truth.

(٦٦) وأما الخامس: وهو الروح القدسى النبوى المنسوب إلى الأولياء إذا كان في غاية الصفاء والشرف

(٦٧) وكانت الروح المفكرة منقسمة إلى ما يحتاج إلى تعليم وتنبيه ومدد من خارج حتى يستمر في أنواع المعارف، وبعضها يكون في شدة الصفاء كأنه يتنبه بنفسه من غير مدد من خارج، فبالحرِىّ أن يعّبر عن الصافي البالغ الاستعداد بأنه يكاد زيته يضيء، ولو لم تمسسه نار: إذ من الأولياء من يكاد يشرق نوره حتى يكاد يستغنى عن مدد الأنبياء؛ وفي الأنبياء من يكاد يستغنى عن مدد الملائكة. فهذا المثال موافق لهذا القسم

(٦٨) وإذا كانت هذه الأنوار مترتبة بعضها على بعض: فالحسى هو الأول؛ وهو كالتوطئة والتمهيد للخيالى، إذ لا يتصور الخيالى إلا موضوعاً بعده؛ والفكرى والعقلى يكونان بعدهما؛ فبالحرى أن تكون الزجاجة كالمحل للمصباح والمشكاة كالمحل للزجاجة: فيكون المصباح في زجاجة، والزجاجة في مشكاة.وإذ كانت هذه كلها أنواراً بعضها فوق بعض فبالحرِىّ أن تكون نوراً على نور.

خاتمة

(٦٩) هذا المثال إنما يتضح لقلوب المؤمنين أو لقلوب الأنبياء والأولياء لا لقلوب الكفار: فإن النور يراد للهداية. فالمصروف عن طريق الهدى باطل وظلمة، بل أشد من الظلمة؛ لأن الظلمة لا تهدى إلى الباطل كما لا تهدى إلى الحق.

(70) The rational faculties of the unbelievers are inverted, and so are the rest of their faculties of perception, and these faculties help one another in leading them astray. Hence, a similitude of them is like a man "in a fathomless ocean covered by a wave above which is a wave above which are clouds, darknesses piled one upon the other" [24:40]. The "ocean" and the "fathomless" are this world, because within it are destructive dangers, harmful occupations, and blinding murkiness.

(71) The first "wave" is the wave of the appetites which call out to the bestial attributes, occupation with sensory pleasures, and achievement of the wishes of this world, so that people will eat and enjoy just as cattle eat. It is appropriate that this wave be something dark, because "love for a thing makes blind and deaf."[19]

(72) The second "wave" is the wave of the attributes of predatoriness, which send forth anger, enmity, hatred, malice, envy, boastfulness, vainglory, and arrogance. It is appropriate that it be something dark, because anger is the ghoul of the rational faculty. And it is appropriate that this be the higher wave, because more often than not anger takes control away from the appetites so that, when one is furious, this distracts from the appetites and makes one heedless of the appetitive pleasures. However, appetite can never overcome a furious anger.

(73) As for "clouds," they are the loathsome beliefs, lying opinions, and corrupt imaginings that have veiled the unbelievers from faith, knowledge of the Real, and the gaining of brightness through the light of the sun of the Qurʾān and the rational faculty. The specific characteristic of clouds is that they veil the radiance of sunlight. Since each of these is something dark, it is appropriate that they be "darknesses piled one upon the other" [24:40].

(74) Since these darknesses veil the knowledge of nearby things—to say nothing of faraway things—this explains why unbelievers are veiled from knowing the wonders of the states of the Prophet, despite

(٧٠) وعقول الكفار انتكست، وكذلك سائر إدراكاتهم وتعاونت على الإضلال في حقهم. فمثالهم كرجل في «بحر لجى يغشاه موج من فوقه موج من فوقه سحاب ظلمات بعضها فوق بعض». والبحر واللّجىّ هو الدنيا بما فيها من الأخطار المهلكة والأشغال المردية والكدورات المعمية.

(٧١) والموج الأول موج الشهوات الداعية إلى الصفات البهيمية والاشتغال باللذات الحسية وقضاء الأوطار الدنيوية، حتى [إنهم] يأكلون ويتمتعون كما تأكل الأنعام. وبالحرِىّ أن يكون هذا الموج مظلماً لأن حب الشىء يعمى ويُصم.

(٧٢) والموج الثانى موج الصفات السَّبُعِية الباعثة على الغضب والعداوة والبغضاء والحقد والحسد والمباهاة والتفاخر والتكاثر. وبالحرى أن يكون مظلماً لأن الغضب غول العقل. وبالحرى أن يكون هو الموج الأعلى: لأن الغضب في الأكثر مستول على الشهوات حتى إذا هاج أذهل عن الشهوات وأغفل عن اللذات المشتهاة. وأما الشهوة فلا تقاوم الغضب الهائج أصلاً.

(٧٣) وأما السحاب فهو الاعتقادات الخبيثة، والظنون الكاذبة، والخيالات الفاسدة التى صارت حجباً بين الكافرين وبين الإيمان ومعرفة الحق والاستضاءة بنور شمس القرآن والعقل: فإن خاصية السحاب أن يحجب إشراق نور الشمس. وإذا كانت هذه كلها مظلمة فبالحرى أن تكون ظلمات بعضها فوق بعض.

(٧٤) وإذا كانت هذه الظلمات تحجب عن معرفة الأشياء القريبة فضلاً عن البعيدة، ولذلك حجب الكفار عن معرفة عجائب أحوال النبى عليه السلام

the nearness of his availability and his manifestation with the least pondering. Hence, it is appropriate that this be referred to with [these words:] "When he puts forth his hand, you can hardly see it" [24:40].

(75) Since the source of all lights is the First Light, the Real—as was clarified earlier—then it is appropriate that each person who has realized the unity of God believe firmly that "to whomsoever God assigns no light, no light has he" [24:40]. This amount of the mysteries of this verse is sufficient for you, so be satisfied with it.

مع قرب متناوله وظهوره بأدنى تأمل، فبالحرى أن يعبر عنه بأنه لوأخرج يده لم يكد يراها.

(٧٥) وإذا كان منبع الأنوار كلها من النور الأول الحق كما سبق بيانه، فبالحرى أن يعتقد كل موحد أن «من لم يجعل الله له نوراً فما له من نور». فيكفيك هذا القدر من أسرار هذه الآية فاقنع به.

The Third Chapter

Concerning the meaning of the Prophet's words:
"God has seventy veils of light and darkness;
were He to lift them, the august glories of His face
would burn up everyone whose eyesight perceived Him"

(1) One version [of this *ḥadīth*] has "seven hundred veils" while another has "seventy thousand." I say:

(2) God discloses Himself to His Essence in His Essence. Without doubt, the "veil" is understood in relation to the thing that is veiled. The veiled among the creatures are of three kinds: those who are veiled by darkness alone, those who are veiled by sheer light, and those who are veiled by light along with darkness.

(3) The types of these kinds are many, and I will verify their multiplicity. With difficulty, I could probably confine them to seventy; but I put no confidence in the delineation and confinement that appear to me, since I do not know whether or not this is what is meant by the *ḥadīth.* As for confining them to seven hundred or seventy thousand, only the prophetic faculty can do that, although it is apparent—it seems to me—that these numbers are mentioned to indicate multiplicity, not to delineate. It is often customary to mention a number not with the desire to confine, but rather to indicate multiplicity. And God knows best the verification of this, for that is outside human capacity. The only thing I can do now is to acquaint you with these kinds and with some of the types of each kind.[1] Hence, I say:

الفصل الثالث

في معنى قوله عليه السلام: «إن لله سبعين حجاباً من نور وظلمة لو كشفها لأحرقت سُبُحَات وجهه كل من أدركه بصرة»

(١) وفي بعض الروايات سبعمائة، وفي بعضها سبعين ألفاً: فأقول:

(٢) إن الله تعالى متجلٍّ في ذاته لذاته، ويكون الحجاب بالإضافة إلى محجوب لا محالة؛ وإن المحجوبين من الخلق ثلاثة أقسام: منهم من حجب بمجرد الظلمة؛ ومنهم من حجب بالنور المحض؛ ومنهم من حجب بنور مقرون بظلمة

(٣) وأصناف هذه الأقسام كثيرة أتحقق كثرتها، ويمكنني أن أتكلف حصرها في سبعين، لكن لاأثق بما يلوح لى من تحديد وحصر، إذ لا أدرى أنه المراد بالحديث أم لا. أما الحصر إلى سبعمائة وسبعين ألفاً فذلك لا يستقل به إلا القوة النبوية، مع أن ظاهر ظنى أن هذه الأعداد مذكورة للتكثير لا للتحديد؛ وقد تجرى العادة بذكر عدد ولا يراد به الحصر بل التكثير. والله أعلم بتحقيق ذلك، فذلك خارج عن الوسع. وإنما الذى يمكننى الآن أن أعرفك هذه الأقسام وبعض أصناف كل قسم فأقول:

The first kind

(4) They are veiled by sheer darkness. They are the atheists, those who do not have faith in God and the Last Day. They love life in this world more than the next world because they do not have faith in the next world at all. These people are of two types.

(5) One type look [for their fulfillment by] searching for the cause of the world. Hence, they turn it over to nature. But nature consists of a quality firmly embedded and adhering in bodies. Bodies are dark, because they do not have knowledge and perception. They have no awareness of themselves and of what proceeds from them, and they have no light perceptible to outward eyesight.

(6) The second type are occupied with themselves and do not attend to searching for the cause [of the world]. Rather, they live the life of the beasts. Their veil is their murky souls and dark appetites. There is no darkness more intense than caprice and the soul. That is why God said, "Hast thou seen him who has taken caprice to be his god?" [25:43]. And the messenger of God said, "Caprice is the most hateful god worshipped on earth."[2]

(7) The second type are divided into groups. One group supposes that the ultimate end of searching in this world is to achieve wishes, to obtain objects of appetite, and to attain bestial pleasures by means of women, food, and clothing.[3] These people are the servants of pleasure. They worship it, search for it, and believe firmly that obtaining it is the highest felicity. They are pleased for their souls to be on the level of the beasts—or, rather, more debased than the beasts. What darkness is more intense than that? Hence, these people have been veiled by sheer darkness.

(8) Another group [of the second type] sees the highest felicity in domination, taking control, killing, capturing, and imprisoning. This is the path of the nomads, Kurds, and many stupid people. They are veiled by

القسم الأول

(٤) وهم المحجوبون بمحض الظلمة، وهم الملحدة الذين لا يؤمنون بالله واليوم الآخر. وهم الذين استحبوا الحياة الدنيا على الآخرة لأنهم لا يؤمنون بالآخرة أصلاً وهؤلاء صنفان:

(٥) صنف تشوّف إلى طلب سبب لهذا العالم فأحاله إلى الطبع: والطبع عبارة عن صفة مركوزة في الأجسام حالّة فيها؛ وهى مظلمة إذ ليس لها معرفة وإدراك ولا خبر لها من نفسها ولا مما يصدر منها؛ وليس لها نور يدرك بالبصر الظاهر أيضاً.

(٦) والصنف الثانى: هم الذين شغلوا بأنفسهم ولم يفرغوا لطلب السبب أيضاً، بل عاشوا عيش البهائم، فكان حجابهم نفوسهم الكدرة، وشهواتهم المظلمة، ولا ظلمة أشد من الهوى والنفس: ولذلك قال الله تعالى: «أفرأيت من اتخذ إلهه هواه» وقال [رسول الله صلى الله عليه وسلم] «الهوى أبغض إله عبد في الأرض».

(٧) وهؤلاء انقسموا فرقاً: فرقة زعمت أن غاية الطلب في الدنيا هى قضاء الأوطار ونيل الشهوات وإدراك اللذات البهيمية من منكح ومطعم وملبس. فهؤلاء عبيد اللذة، يعبدونها ويطلبونها ويعتقدون أن نيلها غاية السعادات: رضوا لأنفسهم أن يكونوا بمنزلة البهائم بل أخس منها. وأى ظلمة أشد من ذلك؟ فقد حجب هؤلاء بمحض الظلمة.

(٨) وفرقة رأت أن غاية السعادات هى الغلبة والاستيلاء والقتل والسبى والأسْر، وهذا مذهب الأعراب والأكراد وكثير من الحمق، وهم محجوبون بظلمة

the darkness of the predatory attributes because these attributes rule over them and because, when these attributes attain their goal, that is the greatest of pleasures. These people are satisfied to be at the level of predatory animals, or even more debased.

(9) A third group [of the second type] sees the highest felicity in the abundance of property and the extension of ease. After all, property is an instrument to achieve the object of appetite. Through it, the human being attains the ability to achieve wishes. Hence, these people aspire to gather property; to increase estates, land, valuable horses, cattle, and farmland, and to hoard dinars in the earth. Hence, you will see one of them striving throughout life—embarking on great dangers in the deserts, on journeys, and in the oceans to gather possessions with which he is niggardly toward himself, to say nothing of others. These are the ones meant by the words of the Prophet: "The slave of the dirham is miserable; the slave of the dinar is miserable."[4] What darkness is greater than that which deceives the human being? Gold and silver are two stones that are not desired in themselves. When wishes are not achieved through them and they are not spent, then they are just like pebbles, and pebbles are just like them.

(10) A fourth group [of the second type] climbs from the ignorance of these people and pretends to possess the rational faculty. They suppose that the highest felicity is the expansion of honor and fame, the spread of reputation, a multiplicity of followers, and the influence of the command that is obeyed. Hence, you see that their only concern is eye service and cultivation of the things upon which observers cast their glance. One of them may go hungry in his house and suffer harm so that he can spend his wealth on clothes with which to adorn himself so that no one will look at him with the eye of contempt when he goes out. The types of these people are beyond count. All of them are veiled from God by the sheer darkness that is their own dark souls.

(11) There is no sense mentioning each and every one of the groups after calling attention to their [general] kinds.

(12) Included among these people is a community that says with their tongues, "There is no god but God." However, it may happen that fear causes them to say this, or they do so to show off and adorn themselves to the Muslims, or to seek provisions from their wealth, or

الصفات السَّبُعية لغلبتها عليهم وكون إدراكها مقصودَها أعظم اللذات. وهؤلاء قنعوا بأن يكونوا بمنزلة السباع بل أخس.

(٩) وفرقة ثالثة رأت أن غاية السعادات كثرة المال واتساع اليسار لأن المال هو آلة قضاء الشهوات كلها، وبه يحصل للإنسان الاقتدار على قضاء الأوطار. فهؤلاء همتهم جمع المال واستكثار الضياع والعقار والخيل المسوّمة والأنعام والحرث وكنز الدنانير تحت الأرض. فترى الواحد يجتهد طول عمره يركب الأخطار في البوادى والأسفار والبحار ويجمع الأموال ويشح بها على نفسه فضلاً عن غيره: وهم المرادون بقوله عليه السلام: «تَعِس عبد الدراهم، تعس عبد الدنانير». وأى ظلمة أعظم مما يُلبّس على الإنسان؟ إن الذهب والفضة حجران لا يرادان لأعيانهما. وهى إذا لم يقض بها الأوطار ولم تنفق فهى والحصباء بمثابة، والحصباء بمثابتها.

(١٠) وفرقة رابعة ترقت عن جهالة هؤلاء وتعاقلت، وزعمت أن أعظم السعادات في اتساع الجاه والصيت وانتشار الذكر وكثرة الأتباع ونفوذ الأمر المطاع. فتراها لاهمّ لها إلا المراءاة وعمارة مطارح أبصار الناظرين: حتى إن الواحد قد يجوع في بيته ويحتمل الضر ويصرف ماله إلى ثياب يتجمل بها عند خروجه كى لا ينظر إليه بعين الحقارة. وأصناف هؤلاء لا يحصون، وكلهم محجوبون عن الله تعالى بمحض الظلمة وهى نفوسهم المظلمة.

(١١) ولا معنى لذكر آحاد الفِرَق بعد وقوع التنبيه على الأجناس.

(١٢) ويدخل في جملة هؤلاء جماعة يقولون بلسانهم «لا إله إلا الله»، لكن ربما حملهم على ذلك خوف أو استظهار بالمسلمين وتجمل بهم أو استمداد من

to be zealous in helping the religion of their fathers. If this saying does not cause these people to do good works, then it does not bring them out of the darknesses into light. Rather, "their protectors are idols, that bring them out from the light into the darknesses" [2:257]. As for one in whom the saying has an effect so that his ugly act is ugly to him and his beautiful act makes him happy, then he comes out from pure darkness, even if he performs many acts of disobedience.

The second kind

(13) They are a company of people veiled by light along with darkness, and they are of three types: a type whose darkness grows out of the senses, a type whose darkness grows out of the imagination, and a type whose darkness grows out of corrupt rational comparisons.

(14) The first type are those veiled by sensory darkness. They [comprise] several companies of people, none of whom fails to pass beyond attending to his own soul to strive at becoming godlike and to look forward to knowledge of his lord. The first of their degrees is the worship of idols; the last of them is dualism; and between [these] two are many degrees.[5]

(15) The first company of people [just mentioned] are the worshippers of idols. They know in a general way that they have a lord whom they must prefer over their dark souls. They believe firmly that their lord is mightier than everything. However, the darkness of the senses veils them from passing beyond the world perceived by the senses. Hence, they make from the most precious of substances—like gold, silver, and rubies—figures formed in the most beautiful of forms, and then take them as gods. These people are veiled by the light of might and beauty. Might and beauty are among the attributes of God and His lights. However, they affix these attributes to bodies perceived by the senses. The darkness of the senses blocks them from [knowing] this because—as was said earlier—compared to the spiritual, rational world, sensory perception is dark.[6]

مالهم؛ أو لأجل التعصب لنصرة مذهب الآباء. فهؤلاء إذا لم تحملهم هذه الكلمة على العمل الصالح فلا تخرجهم الكلمة من الظلمات إلى النور، بل «أولياؤهم الطاغوت يخرجونهم من النور إلى الظلمات». أما من أثرت فيه الكلمة بحيث ساءته سيئته وسرته حسنته فهو خارج عن محض الظلمة وإن كان كثير المعصية.

القسم الثانى

(١٣) طائفة حجبوا بنور مقرون بظلمة وهم ثلاثة أصناف: صنف منشأ ظلمتهم من الحس، وصنف منشأ ظلمتهم من الخيال، وصنف منشأ ظلمتهم من مقايسات عقلية فاسدة.

(١٤) الصنف الأول المحجوبون بالظلمة الحسية، وهم طوائف لا يخلو واحد منهم عن مجاوزة الالتفات إلى نفسه وعن التأله والتشوف إلى معرفة ربه. وأول درجاتهم عبدة الأوثان وآخرهم الثنوية، وبينهما درجات.

(١٥) فالطائفة الأولى عبدة الأوثان: علموا على الجملة أن لهم رباً يلزمهم إيثاره على نفوسهم المظلمة، واعتقدوا أن ربهم أعز من كل شيء ولكن حجبتهم ظلمة الحس عن أن يجاوزوا العالم المحسوس فاتخذوا من أنفس الجواهر كالذهب والفضة والياقوت أشخاصاً مصورة بأحسن الصور واتخذوها آلهة. فهؤلاء محجوبون بنور العزة والجمال. والعزة والجمال من صفات الله وأنواره، ولكنهم ألصقوها بالأجسام المحسوسة وصدهم عن ذلك ظلمة الحس، فإن الحس ظلمة بالإضافة إلى العالم الروحانى العقلى كما سبق.

(16) The second company of people are a community of the furthest Turks. They have neither a religious creed nor a revealed law, and they believe firmly that they have a lord and that he is the most beautiful of things. When they see a human having the utmost degree of beauty—or a tree, or a horse, or something else—they prostrate themselves before it and say, "This is our lord!" These people are veiled by the light of beauty, along with the darkness of the senses. They are more able to enter into observing light than the worshippers of idols because they worship beauty that is not limited to a specific individual. They do not single out any specific thing for beauty. Moreover, they worship natural beauty, not what is made for them and by their own hands.

(17) A third company of people say, "Our lord must be luminous in his own essence, splendid in his form, possessor of authority in himself, awe-inspiring in his presence, and unbearable to be near." However, he must be perceived by the senses because, in their view, what is not perceived by the senses has no meaning. Then they find that fire has this quality and they worship it, taking it as a lord. They are veiled by the lights of ruling authority and splendor, which are among the lights of God.[7]

(18) A fourth company of people suppose as follows: "We take control of fire through lighting and extinguishing flames, so it is under our free disposal and is not fitting for divinity. On the contrary, that which is [fitting for divinity] has these attributes and [yet] is not under our free disposal, though we are under its free disposal; and it is also described by highness and elevation." At the same time, the sciences of celestial bodies and of the influences ascribed to these bodies are well known among them. Hence, some of these people worship Sirius, some worship Jupiter, and some worship other stars, in keeping with the many influences that they firmly believe to be in the celestial bodies. All of them are veiled by the lights of highness, radiance, and taking control, which are among the lights of God.

(19) A fifth company support the approach of those people but say, "Our lord must not be branded by smallness and largeness in relation to the many luminous substances; rather, he must be the greatest of

(١٦) الطائفة الثانية جماعة من أقاصى الترك ليس لهم ملة ولا شريعة يعتقدون أن لهم رباً وأنه أجملُ الأشياء، فإذا رأوا إنساناً في غاية الجمال أو شجراً أو فَرَساً أو غير ذلك سجدوا له وقالوا إنه ربنا. فهؤلاء محجوبون بنور الجمال مع ظلمة الحس، وهم أدخل في ملاحظة النور من عبدة الأوثان لأنهم يعبدون الجمال المطلق دون الشخص الخاص فلا يخصصونه بشيء؛ ثم يعبدون الجمال المطبوع لا المصنوع من جهتهم وبأيديهم.

(١٧) وطائفة ثالثة قالوا ينبغى أن يكون ربنا نورانياً في ذاته بهيّاً في صورته، ذا سلطان في نفسه، مهيباً في حضرته، لا يطاق القرب منه، ولكن ينبغى أن يكون محسوساً؛ إذ لا معنى لغير المحسوس عندهم. ثم وجدوا النار بهذه الصفة فعبدوها واتخذوها رباً. فهؤلاء محجوبون بنور السلطنة والبهاء: وكل ذلك من أنوار الله تعالى.

(١٨) وطائفة رابعة زعموا أن النار نستولى عليها نحن بالإشعال والإطفاء، فهى تحت تصرفنا فلا تصلح للإلهية، بل ما يكون بهذه الصفات ولم يكن تحت تصرفنا ثم نكون نحن تحت تصرفه ويكون مع ذلك موصوفاً بالعلو والارتفاع. ثم كان المشهور فيما بينهم علم النجوم وإضافة التأثيرات إليها. فمنهم من عبد الشِّعرَى، ومنهم من عبد المُشْتَرى إلى غير ذلك من الكواكب بحسب ما اعتقدوه في النجوم من كثرة التأثيرات. فهؤلاء محجوبون بنور العلو والإشراق والاستيلاء، وهى من أنوار الله تعالى.

(١٩) وطائفة خامسة ساعدت هؤلاء في المأخذ ولكن قالت لا ينبغى أن يكون ربنا موسوماً بالصغر والكِبَر بالإضافة إلى الجواهر النورانية، بل ينبغى

them." Hence, they worship the sun, saying, "She is greater!" They are veiled by the light of magnificence, together with the remaining lights, and with the darkness of sensory perception.

(20) A sixth company climb beyond these people and say, "The sun does not possess all light alone, since others also have lights. And it is not appropriate that the lord have a partner in his luminosity." Hence, they worship unlimited light, which brings together all the lights of the world. They suppose that this is the lord of the world and that all good things are ascribed to it. Then they saw that there is evil in the world, [and] they did not consider it beautiful to ascribe it to their lord, declaring him devoid of evil. Thus, they set up a struggle between their lord and darkness, and they turn the world over to light and darkness. Sometimes they call the two Yazdān and Ahriman.[8] These are the dualists.

(21) This amount is sufficient to alert you to this first type, who are many more than these.

(22) The second type are those veiled by some lights along with the darkness of imagination. They are those who have passed beyond the senses. They establish something beyond sensory things, but they are not able to pass beyond imagination. Hence, they worship an existent thing that sits upon the throne.[9]

(23) The most debased of them in level are the Mujassima.[10] Then comes every type of Karrāmiya.[11] It is not possible for me to explain their doctrines and paths, so there is no benefit in listing them. The loftiest of them in degree are those who negate corporeality and all its accidental qualities except the direction specified as "up." This is because something that is not related to directions and is not described as outside or inside the world is not, in their view, an existent thing, since it cannot be imagined. They do not perceive that the first degree of rational objects is to pass beyond ascription to the directions.[12]

(24) The third type are those who are veiled by the divine lights along with dark, corrupt, rational comparisons. They worship a hearing, seeing, speaking, knowing, powerful, desiring, living god who [cannot be described]

أن يكون أكبرها، فعبدوا الشمس وقالوا هى أكبر. فهؤلاء محجوبون بنور الكبرياء مع بقية الأنوار مقروناً بظلمة الحس.

(٢٠) وطائفة سادسة ترقوا عن هؤلاء فقالوا: النور كله لا ينفرد به الشمس بل لغيرها أنوار، ولا ينبغى للرب شريك في نورانيته فعبدوا النور المطلق الجامع لجميع أنوار العالم وزعموا أنه رب العالم والخيرات كلها منسوبة إليه. ثم رأوا في العالم شروراً فلم يستحسنوا إضافتها إلى ربهم تنزيهاً له عن الشر، فجعلوا بينه وبين الظلمة منازعة، وأحالوا العالم إلى النور والظلمة، وربما سموهما «يزدان» و«أهرمن»، وهم الثنوية.

(٢١) فيكفيك هذا القدر تنبيهاً على هذا الصنف، فهم أكثر من ذلك.

(٢٢) الصنف الثانى المحجوبون ببعض الأنوار مقروناً بظلمة الخيال، وهم الذين جاوزا الحس، وأثبتوا وراء المحسوسات أمراً، لكن لم يمكنهم مجاوزة الخيال، فعبدوا موجوداً قاعداً على العرش.

(٢٣) وأخسهم رتبة المجسّمة ثم أصناف الكرّامية بأجمعهم. ولا يمكننى شرح مقالاتهم ومذاهبهم فلا فائدة في التكثير. لكن أرفعهم درجة مَنْ نَفَى الجسمية وجميع عوارضها إلا الجهة المخصوصة بجهة فوق: لأن الذى لا ينسب إلى الجهات ولا يوصف بأنه خارج العالم ولا داخله لم يكن عندهم موجوداً إذ لم يكن متخيلاً. ولم يدركوا أن أول درجات المعقولات تجاوزُ النسبة إلى الجهات.

(٢٤) الصنف الثالث المحجوبون بالأنوار الإلهية مقرونة بمقايسات عقلية فاسدة مظلمة فعبدوا إلها سميعاً بصيراً متكلماً عالماً قادراً مريداً حياً، منزهاً عن

with directions. But they understand these attributes in keeping with how they stand in relation to their own attributes. One of them may say explicitly that his [god's] speech is sounds and letters like our speech. Another may climb higher and say, "No, rather it is like the speech of our own soul—there are neither sounds nor letters." This is why, when the reality of hearing, seeing, and life is demanded from them, they fall back on declaring similarity in respect to the meaning, although verbally they deny the reality, since in no way do they perceive the meanings of these ascriptions in respect to God. This is the reason why they say about His desire, "It is temporally originated, like our desire; it is a seeking and an intending, like our intending." These are well-known doctrines, and there is no need to go into their details.[13]

(25) These people are veiled by a certain amount of the lights together with the darkness of rational comparisons. All of them are types belonging to the second kind, who are veiled by light along with darkness. And God alone grants success.

The third kind

(26) They are veiled by sheer lights. They are of many types, and it is not possible to enumerate them. I will, however, allude to three of their types.

(27) The first is a company of people who come to know the meanings of the attributes through verification. They perceive that ascribing the names "speaking," "desiring," "powerful," "knowing," and so forth to His attributes is not like ascribing them to human beings. They avoid making Him known through these attributes and come to know Him in relation to the creatures, just as Moses made known in answer to the words of Pharaoh: "And what is the Lord of the worlds?" [26:23]. They reply, "The Lord, who is too holy for and incomparable with the meanings of these attributes, is the Mover and Governor of the heavens."[14]

الجهات، لكن فهموا هذه الصفات على حسب مناسبة صفاتهم. وربما صرّح بعضهم فقال: «كلامه صوت وحرف ككلامِنَا». وربما ترقي بعضهم فقال: «لا بل هو كحديث نفسنا ولا هو صوت ولا حرف». وكذلك إذا طولبوا بحقيقة السمع والبصر والحياة رجعوا إلى التشبيه من حيث المعنى وإن أنكروها باللفظ إذ لم يدركوا أصلاً معانى هذه الإطلاقات في حق الله تعالى. ولذلك قالوا في إرادته إنها حادثة مثل إرادتنا. وإنها طلب وقصد مثل قصدنا. وهذه مذاهب مشهورة فلاحاجة إلى تفصيلها.

(٢٥) فهؤلاء محجوبون بجملة من الأنوار مع ظلمة المقايسات العقلية. فهؤلاء كلهم أصناف القسم الثانى الذين حجبوا بنور مقرون بظلمة. وبالله التوفيق.

القسم الثالث

(٢٦) ثم المحجوبون بمحض الأنوار وهم أصناف ولا يمكن إحصاؤهم: فأشير إلى ثلاثة أصناف منهم.

(٢٧) الأول طائفة عرفوا معانى الصفات تحقيقاً وأدركوا أن إطلاق اسم الكلام والإرادة والقدرة والعلم وغيرها على صفاته ليس مثل إطلاقه على البشر؛ فتحاشوا عن تعريفه بهذه الصفات وعرفوه بالإضافة إلى المخلوقات كما عرّف موسى عليه السلام في جواب قول فرعون: «وما رب العالمين» فقالوا إن الرب المقدّس المنزّه عن معانى هذه الصفات هو محرّك السموات ومدبرها.

(28) The second type climbs beyond these people in the respect that it becomes manifest to them that there is multiplicity in the heavens and that the mover of each specific heaven is a different existent thing called an "angel," of whom there are many. The angels' relationship with the divine lights is that of the stars.[15] Furthermore, it appears to these people that these heavens are inside another celestial sphere that moves all of them by its movement once in a day and a night. Hence, the Lord is the mover of the furthest celestial body that envelops all the celestial spheres, since plurality is rejected as pertaining to the Lord.[16]

(29) The third type climbs beyond these and says, "Putting bodies into movement by means of direct contact necessitates that there be a service rendered to the Lord of the worlds: worship of Him, and obedience toward Him by one of His servants, called an angel. The angel's relationship with the sheer divine lights is the relationship of the moon among the sensory lights." They suppose that the Lord is the one who is obeyed in respect of this mover and that the Lord is a mover of everything by means of command, not direct contact. Then, in the classification and quiddity of that command, there is an obscurity before which most understandings fall short and for which this book does not have the capacity.[17]

(30) All these types are veiled by pure light.

(31) "Those who have arrived" are only the fourth type.[18] To them it has been disclosed that the one who is obeyed is described by an attribute that contradicts sheer oneness and utmost perfection. [This] belongs to a mystery which is beyond the capacity of this book to unveil. [It is also disclosed] that the relationship of this one who is obeyed is that of the sun among the lights. Therefore, they have turned their faces from the one who moves the heavens, from the one who moves the furthest celestial body, from the one who commands moving them, to Him who originates the heavens, originates the furthest celestial body, and originates the one who commands moving the heavens. They have arrived at an existent thing that is incomparable with everything that their sight had perceived. Hence, the august glories of His face—the First, the Highest—burn up everything perceived by the sights and insights of the observers. Thus, they find Him too holy for and incomparable with all that we described earlier.

(٢٨) والصنف الثانى ترقوا عن هؤلاء من حيث ظهر لهم أن في السموات كثرة، وأن محرك كلّ سماء خاصة موجود آخر يسمى مَلكا، وفيهم كثرة، وإنما نسبتهم إلى الأنوار الإلهية نسبة الكواكب. ثم لاح لهم أن هذه السموات في ضمن فلك آخر يتحرك الجميع بحركته في اليوم والليلة مرة. فالرب هو المحرك للجِرم الأقصى المنطوى على الأفلاك كلها إذ الكثرة منفية عنه.

(٢٩) والصنف الثالث ترقوا عن هؤلاء وقالوا: إن تحريك الأجسام بطريق المباشرة ينبغى أن يكون خدمة لرب العالمين وعبادة له وطاعة من عبد من عباده يسمى مَلَكا: نسبته إلى الأنوار الإلهية المحضة نسبة القمر في الأنوار المحسوسة. فزعموا أن الرب هو المطاع من جهة هذا المحرّك؛ ويكون الرب تعالى محركاً للكل بطريق الأمر لا بطريق المباشرة. ثم في تقسيم ذلك الأمر وماهيته غموض يقصر عنه أكثر الأفهام ولا يحتمله هذا الكتاب.

(٣٠) فهؤلاء الأصناف كلهم محجوبون بالأنوار المحضة.

(٣١) وإنما الواصلون صنف رابع تجلى لهم أيضاً أن هذا المطاع موصوف بصفة تنافي الوحدانية المحضة والكمال البالغ لسر لا يحتمل هذا الكتاب كشفه: وأن نسبة هذا المطاع نسبة الشمس في الأنوار. فتوجهوا مِن الذى يحرك السموات ومن الذى يحرك الجرم الأقصى، ومِن الذى أمر بتحريكها إلى الذى فطر السموات وفطر الجرم الأقصي وفطر الآمر بتحريكها، فوصلوا إلى موجود منزه عن كل ما أدركه بصرٌ من قبلهم، فأحرقت سبحات وجهه الأول الأعلى جميع ما أدركه بصر الناظرين وبصيرتهم فإذ وَجَدوه مقدساً منزهاً عن جميع ما وصفناه من قبل.

(32) Then they are divided into groups. Everything the sight of one group perceives is burned up, effaced, and annihilated. But they remain, observing the beauty and the holiness while also observing their own essences in the beauty that they attained through arriving at the divine presence. Hence, the objects of vision are effaced, but not the person who sees.

(33) Another group, who are the elect of the elect, pass beyond this. The august glories of His face burn them up, and the ruling authority of majesty overcomes them. In their essences they are effaced and annihilated. They become extinct from themselves, so that they cease observing themselves. Nothing remains save the One, the Real. The meaning of His words, "Everything is perishing except His face" [28:88], becomes for them a taste and a state. We already alluded to this in the first chapter, where we mentioned how they applied the word "unification" and what they thought of it.[19] This is the ultimate end of those who have arrived.

(34) Another group does not climb and ascend according to the details we mentioned. For them the path is not long. At the very beginning they come to know holiness and the declaration of lordship's incomparability, with everything its incomparability necessitates. What dominates over the others at the end dominates over them at the beginning. The revelation of Himself rushes upon them at once, and the august glories of His face burn up everything that sensory sight and rational insight are able to perceive. It is likely that the first path is that of the Friend [Abraham], while the second path is that of the Beloved [Muḥammad].[20] God knows best the mysteries of the steps of these two, and the lights of their station.

(35) Thus have I alluded to the various types of those who are veiled. It is not unlikely that if writings were set forth in detail and the veils of the travelers were traced, their number could reach seventy thousand. But if you investigate, you will not find a single one of them outside the kinds we listed, because people can only be veiled by their human attributes, senses, imagination, comparisons of the rational faculty, or sheer light, as was said earlier.

(٣٢) ثم هؤلاء انقسموا: فمنهم من احترق منه جميع ما أدركه بصره وانمحق وتلاشى، لكن بقى هو ملاحظاً للجمال والقدس وملاحظاً ذاته في جماله الذى ناله بالوصول إلى الحضرة الإلهية. فانمحقت فيه المبصرات دون المبصَر.

(٣٣) وجاوز هؤلاء طائفة هم خواص الخواص فأحرقتهم سبحات وجهه وغشيهم سلطان الجلال فانمحقوا وتلاشوا في ذاتهم ولم يبق لهم لحاظ إلى أنفسهم لفنائهم عن أنفسهم. ولم يبق إلا الواحد الحق. وصار معنى قوله: «كل شيء هالك إلا وجهه» لهم ذوقاً وحالاً. وقد أشرنا إلى ذلك في الفصل الأول، وذكرنا أنهم كيف أطلقوا الاتحاد وكيف ظنوه. فهذه نهاية الواصلين.

(٣٤) ومنهم من لم يتدرج في الترقي والعروج على التفصيل الذى ذكرناه ولم يطُلْ عليهم الطريق فسبقوا في أول وهلة إلى معرفة القدس وتنزيه الربوبية عن كل ما يجب تنزيهه عنه، فغلب عليهم أولاً ماغلب على الآخرين آخراً، وهجم عليهم التجلى دفعة فأحرقت سبحات وجهه جميع ما يمكن أن يدركه بصر حسى وبصيرة عقلية. ويشبه أن يكون الأول طريق «الخليل» والثانى طريق «الحبيب» صلى الله عليه وسلم، والله أعلم بأسرار أقدامهما وأنوار مقامهما.

(٣٥) فهذه إشارة إلى أصناف المحجوبين، ولا يبعد [أن يبلغ] عددهم إذا فصّلت المقالات وتُتُبّع حجب السالكين سبعين ألفاً. ولكن إذا فتشت لا تجد واحداً منها خارجاً عن الأقسام التى حصرناها: فإنهم إنما يحجبون بصفاتهم البشرية، أو بالحس أو بالخيال أو بمقايسة العقل، أو بالنور المحض كما سبق.

(36) This is what readily came to mind in answer to these questions, even though I was asked unexpectedly while my thoughts were divided, my notions diverging, and my concerns turned to a discipline other than this. My request to the questioner is that he ask God to forgive wherever my pen has transgressed and my foot has slipped, because delving into the flood of the divine mysteries is dangerous, and seeking to penetrate the divine lights from behind human veils is arduous, not easy.

(٣٦) فهذا ماحضرنى في جواب هذه الأسئلة، مع أن السؤال صادفنى والفكر متقسم، والخاطر متشعب، والهمُّ إلى غير هذا الفن منصرف. ومقترحى عليه أن يسأل الله تعالى العفو عما طغى به القلم، أو زلّت به القدم؛ فإن خوض غمرة الأسرار الإلهية خطير، واستشفاف الأنوار الإلهية من وراء الحجب البشرية عسير غير يسير.

Notes to the English Text

Abbreviations

References to *ḥadīth* collections in the notes below follow the system employed by A. J. Wensinck in his *Concordance et indices de la tradition musulmane,* 2d ed., 8 vols. (Leiden: E. J. Brill, 1992). That is, for the collections of Abū Daʾūd, al-Bukhārī, Muslim, and al-Tirmidhī, the references include the name of the compiler followed by the name of the book within the compilation and then the number of the *bāb* or tradition. In the case of Aḥmad Ibn Ḥanbal's *Musnad,* a volume number is given followed by a page number, both of which are derived from an edition printed in Cairo in 1895 by an unknown publisher. Subsequent editions of the *Musnad,* published by various houses in a number of countries, have typically retained the pagination of the 1895 Cairo edition. Following are bibliographical references to the *ḥadīth* collections consulted and the abbreviated names by which they are referenced in these notes.

Abū Daʾūd	Abū Daʾūd, Sulaymān ibn al-Ashʿath. *Sunan Abū Daʾūd.* Edited by Aḥmad Saʿd ʿAlī. 2 vols. Cairo: Muṣṭafā al-Bābī al-Ḥalabī, 1952.
Bukhārī	Al-Bukhārī, Muḥammad ibn Ismāʿīl. *Ṣaḥīḥ Abī ʿAbd Allāh al-Bukhārī.* 25 vols. Cairo: Al-Maṭbaʿa al-Bahīya al-Miṣrīya, 1933–62. See also the translation by Muḥammad Muḥsin Khān, *The Translation of the Meanings of Ṣaḥiḥ al-Bukhārī.* 6th rev. ed. 9 vols. Chicago: Kazi Publications, 1983.
Muslim	Muslim ibn al-Ḥajjāj. *Al-Ṣaḥīḥ Muslim.* 8 vols. Cairo: Maktaba wa Maṭbaʿa Muḥammad ʿAlī Sabīh wa Awlādahu, 1963.
Tirmidhī	Al-Tirmidhī, Muḥammad ibn ʿĪsā. *Ṣaḥīḥ bi-sharḥ al-imām Ibn alʿArabī al-Mālikī.* 13 vols. Cairo: n.p., 1931–34.
Aḥmad	Ibn Ḥanbal, Aḥmad. *Musnad.* 6 vols. Cairo: n.p., 1895.

Translator's Introduction

1. See Gairdner's introduction to his translation of *The Niche of Lights:* al-Ghazālī, *Mishkāt al-Anwār (The Niche for Lights)*, trans. W. H. T. Gairdner (1924; reprint, Lahore, Pakistan: Sh. Muḥammad Ashraf, 1952), 2; and ᶜAfīfī's introduction to his edition: al-Ghazālī, *Mishkāt al-anwār,* ed. Abū al-ᶜAlā ᶜAfīfī (Cairo: Al-Dār al-Qawmīya lil-Tabāᶜa wa al-Nashar, 1964), 4.

2. All quotations from the Qurᵓān are based on A. J. Arberry's *The Koran Interpreted* (New York: Macmillan, 1955). References to the Qurᵓān will follow the quote, the first number indicating the chapter and the second number the verse. Some of Arberry's translations have been modified to fit better into al-Ghazālī's discussions. The translation of the Veils *Ḥadīth* is my own.

3. Many scholars see *The Niche of Lights* as primarily a Ṣūfī text. See Gairdner's "Al-Ghazālī's *Mishkāt al-Anwār* and the Ghazālī Problem," *Der Islam* 5 (1914): 121–53; A. J. Wensinck's "On the Relation between Ghazālī's Cosmology and His Mysticism," *Mededelingen der koninklijke Akademe van Wetenschappen, Afdeling Letterkunde* 75 (series A), no. 6 (1933): 183–209, and his "Ghazālī's *Mishkāt al-Anwār (Niche of Lights),*" in *Semietische Studien: Uit de Nalatenschap* (Leiden: A. W. Sijthoff's Uitgeversmaatschappij N.V., 1941); and Hava Lazarus-Yafeh's *Studies in al-Ghazzālī* (Jerusalem: Magnes Press, 1975).

4. For a concise and thorough introduction to *ḥadīth* literature in Islamic religious thought, see M. A. Siddīqi's *Ḥadīth Literature: Its Origin, Development, and Special Features* (Cambridge: Islamic Texts Society, 1993). References to *ḥadīth* will include traditional sources and Wensinck's *Concordance et indices de la tradition musulmane,* 2d ed., 8 vols. (Leiden: E. J. Brill, 1992). If these sources prove unhelpful, reference will also be made to al-Ghazālī's *Iḥyāᵓ ᶜulūm al-dīn* (The revivification of the religious sciences), 5 vols. (Beirut: Dār al-Hādī, 1992).

5. On the authority of al-Ghazālī, see the quotations compiled by Richard Joseph McCarthy, translator of the recent English edition of al-Ghazālī's autobiography: al-Ghazālī, *Freedom and Fulfillment: An Annotated Translation of al-Ghazālī's* Al-Munqidh min al-Dalāl *and Other Relevant Works of al-Ghazālī,* trans. Richard Joseph McCarthy (Boston: Twayne, 1980), xii–xiii.

6. One sound *ḥadīth* relates that "at the beginning of every hundred years someone belonging to that time will renew its religion *(dīnahā)*." See Wensinck, *Concordance* 1: 324; and Abū Daᵓūd, Malāḥim, 1. During al-Ghazālī's lifetime, many considered him the "renewer" of his age. See W. Montgomery Watt's article, "Al-Ghazālī, Abū Ḥāmid," in *The Encyclopedia of Religion* (New York: Macmillan, 1987), 5: 541–44.

7. Some important studies in English on al-Ghazālī's life and writings include, in chronological order, D. B. Macdonald, "The Life of al-Ghazzālī, with Especial Reference to His Religious Experiences and Opinions," *Journal of the American Oriental Society* 20 (1899): 71–132; W. R. W. Gardner, *An Account of al-Ghazālī's Life and Works* (Madras: n.p., 1919); Samuel Zwemer, *A Moslem Seeker after God: Showing Islam at Its Best in the Life and Teaching of al-Ghazali, Mystic and Theologian of the Eleventh Century* (New York: Fleming H. Revell, 1920); Margaret Smith, *Al-Ghazālī the Mystic* (1944; reprint, Lahore, Pakistan: Hijra International, 1983); W. Montgomery Watt's two well-known books, *The*

Faith and Practice of al-Ghazālī (London: G. Allen and Unwin, 1953) and *Muslim Intellectual: A Study of al-Ghazālī* (Edinburgh: Edinburgh University Press, 1963); Lazarus-Yafeh, *Studies in Al-Ghazzālī;* and McCarthy's introduction to his translation of al-Ghazālī's *Freedom and Fulfillment.* McCarthy's book also contains a thorough annotated bibliography of important studies on and translations of al-Ghazālī's writings up to the late 1970s.

Two concise summaries of the life and works of al-Ghazālī and of his significance in Islamic philosophy are W. Montgomery Watt's "Al-Ghazālī, Abū Ḥāmid Muḥammad b. Muḥammad al-Ṭūṣī," in *The Encyclopedia of Islam,* new ed. (Leiden: E. J. Brill, 1965), 2:1038–41; and M. Saeed Sheikh, "Al-Ghazālī," in *A History of Muslim Philosophy: With Short Accounts of Other Disciplines and the Modern Renaissance in Muslim Lands,* ed. M. M. Sharif (Wiesbaden: Otto Harrassowitz, 1963), 1: 581–624, 637–42.

Recent translations of other works by al-Ghazālī include *The Precious Pearl: A Translation from the Arabic, with Notes, of the* Kitāb al-Durra al-Fākhira fī Kashf ʿUlūm al-Ākhira *of Abū Ḥāmid Muḥammad b. Muḥammad b. Muḥammad al-Ghazālī,* trans. and ed. Jane Idleman Smith, Harvard University Studies in World Religion, no. 1 (Missoula, Montana: Scholars Press, 1979); *Invocations and Supplications: Kitāb al-Adhkār wa 'l-Daʿawāt, Book IX of* The Revival of the Religious Sciences, Ihyāʾ ʿUlūm al-Dīn, trans. K. Nakamura, rev. ed. (Cambridge: Islamic Texts Society, 1990; originally published as *Ghazālī on Prayer,* Tokyo: University of Tokyo, 1973); and *The Remembrance of Death and the Afterlife (Kitāb Dhikr al-Mawt wa-Mā Baʿduhu), Book XL of* The Revival of the Religious Sciences, Ihyāʾ ʿUlūm al-Dīn, trans. T. J. Winter (Cambridge: Islamic Texts Society, 1989).

8. For a chronological listing of the 404 works attributed to al-Ghazālī, see P. Bouyges, *Essai de chronologie des oeuvres de al-Ghazali,* ed. M. Allard (Beirut: n.p., 1959); and G. F. Hourani, "The Chronology of Ghazālī's Writing," *Journal of the American Oriental Society* 89 (1959): 225–33.

9. For example, in Islamic theology *(kalām)* al-Ghazālī's chief works are *Al-iqtiṣād fī al-iʿtiqād* (The golden mean of belief) and *Iljām al-ʿawwām ʿan ʿilm al-kalām* (Restraining the common people from the science of theology); in law *(fiqh)* they are *Al-basīṭ fī furūʿ al-madhhab* (A simple discussion of the branches of the school of law) and *Al-mustaṣfā fī uṣūl al-fiqh* (A clear discussion of the principles of jurisprudence); and in philosophy *(falsafa)* they are the famous *Maqāṣid al-falāsifa* (The intentions of the philosophers) and *Tahāfut al-falāsifa* (The incoherence of the philosophers).

Some chapters of al-Ghazālī's *Al-iqtiṣād fī al-iʿtiqād* have been translated into English. See *Al-Ghazālī on Divine Predicates and Their Properties: A Critical and Annotated Translation of These Chapters in* Al-Iqtiṣād fil-Iʿtiqād, trans. ʿAbdu-r-Raḥmān Abū Zayd (1970; reprint, Lahore, Pakistan: Sh. Muḥammad Ashraf, 1974). For translations of *Tahāfut al-falāsifa,* see note 19 below.

10. For a discussion of Ṣūfism's emphasis on actualizing these three dimensions of law, faith, and virtue in the interpretation of Islam, see William C. Chittick, *The Faith and Practice of Islam: Three Thirteenth Century Sufi Texts* (Albany: State University of New York Press, 1992), 1–33; Sachiko Murata and William C. Chittick, *The Vision of Islam* (New York: Paragon House, 1994);

and Louis Brenner, "Concepts of Ṭarīqa in West Africa: The Case of the Qādiriyya," in *Charisma and Brotherhood in African Islam,* ed. Donal B. Cruise O'Brien and Christian Coulon (Oxford: Clarendon Press, 1988), 33–36.

11. Little is known of the life of Aḥmad al-Ghazālī (d. 1126), the younger brother of the more well-known Abū Ḥāmid. We do know that Aḥmad was an accomplished scholar because he was capable of taking over his brother's prestigious teaching post when the latter abandoned it to devote the rest of his life to purifying his heart. Aḥmad was also an accomplished Ṣūfī master. In the Persian-speaking world he is best known for his classical Ṣūfī treatise on the metaphysics of love, *Al-sawāniḥ,* which "establish[es] him as one of the greatest mystics in the Muslim world" (Annemarie Schimmel, *Mystical Dimensions of Islam* [Chapel Hill: University of North Carolina Press, 1975], 295). For a translation see Aḥmad Al-Ghazālī, *Sawanih: Inspirations from the World of Pure Spirits: The Oldest Persian Sufi Treatise on Love,* trans. Nasrollah Pourjavady (London: KPI, 1986). For further biographical information, see H. Ritter's article, "Al-Ghazālī, Aḥmad B. Muḥammad," in *The Encyclopaedia of Islam,* new ed. (Leiden: E. J. Brill, 1965), 2:1041–42.

12. W. Montgomery Watt, *Islamic Philosophy and Theology* (Edinburgh: Edinburgh University Press, 1962), 85.

13. One of al-Ghazālī's contributions to this subject, as seen in his *Al-iqtiṣād fī al-iᶜtiqād* (The golden mean of belief), was to add a more sophisticated philosophical argument to theology through the use of the syllogism (ibid., 118). Toward the end of his life he wrote *Iljām al-ᶜawwām ᶜan ᶜilm al-kalām* (Restraining the common people from the science of theology), in which he severely criticizes theological discussions. Here he felt that the theological method limited knowledge of God to a purely rationalistic way of knowing. To a large degree, theology implicitly denied the possibility of a direct inner knowledge of God. Perhaps one of the reasons he felt that *kalām* should not be learned by everyone is that people might become too attached to a purely rational way of knowing God. Hence, they would disregard the inherent human ability to actualize divine knowledge directly in the heart.

14. See Carl Brockelmann and L. Gardet, "Al-Djuwaynī, Abū 'l-Maᶜālī ᶜAbd al-Malik," in *The Encyclopaedia of Islam,* new ed. (Leiden: E. J. Brill, 1965), 2:605–6.

15. See note 9 above.

16. See M. G. S. Hodgson, "Bāṭinīya," in *The Encyclopaedia of Islam,* new ed. (Leiden: E. J. Brill, 1960) 1:1098; and Watt, *Islamic Philosophy and Theology,* 119.

17. Al-Ghazālī's polemic against the Bāṭinite doctrine includes works such as *Al-mustaẓhirī fī radd ᶜalā al-bāṭinīya* (The book dedicated to sultan Mustaẓhir concerning a reply to the Bāṭinites) and *Al-qusṭās al-mustaqīm* (The just balance). See Watt, *Muslim Intellectual,* 74–82. For an English translation of *Al-qusṭās,* see "Appendix III: *Al-Qusṭās al-Mustaqīm,*" in McCarthy, *Freedom and Fulfillment,* 287–332.

18. See Saeed Sheikh, "Al-Ghazālī," 593.

19. For English translations of *Tahāfut al-falāsifa,* see al-Ghazālī, *The Incoherence of the Philosophers,* trans. Michael E. Marmura, Islamic Translation Series (Provo, Utah: Brigham Young University Press, 1997); and Ibn Rushd,

Averroës' Tahafut al-Tahafut, trans. S. van den Bergh (London: n.p., 1954), in which Ibn Rushd incorporates al-Ghazālī's *Tahāfut al-falāsifa* into his refutation of that work.

20. See Majid Fakhry, *A History of Islamic Philosophy,* 2d ed. (New York: Columbia University Press, 1983), 293–311.

21. See ᶜAfīfī's edition of *Mishkāt,* 34–35; and Hermann Landolt, "Ghazālī and *'Religionswissenschaft'*: Some Notes on the *Mishkāt al-Anwār* for Professor Charles J. Adams," *Asiatische Studien (Etudes asiatiques)* 45, no. 1 (1991): 59.

22. See Saeed Sheikh, "Al-Ghazālī," 594.

23. For a summary of various Islamic interpretations of the heart, soul, spirit, and intellect, see Sachiko Murata's *The Tao of Islam: A Sourcebook on Gender Relationships in Islamic Thought* (Albany: State University of New York Press, 1992), 232–41 and chapter 10.

24. For discussions of the inherent relationship of Ṣūfism to other dimensions of Islamic thought and practice, see Chittick, *Faith and Practice of Islam,* especially parts 1 and 4; and Mark Woodward, *Islam in Java: Normative Piety and Mysticism in the Sultanate of Yogyakarta* (Tucson: University of Arizona Press, 1989) 4–8, 60–66, in which he provides a summary of the various arguments in Islamic studies on this relationship.

25. See William C. Chittick, "Dhikr," in *Encyclopedia of Religion* (New York: Macmillan, 1987), 4:341–44.

26. This is seen in early Arabic treatises which are still published, such as al-Qushayrī's *Risāla* and al-Makkī's *Qūt al-qulūb.* English translations of compilations of this genre can be found in Dr. Javad Nurbakhsh's Ṣūfism series. For example, see *Sufism IV: Repentance, Abstinence, Renunciation, Wariness, Humility, Humbleness, Sincerity, Constancy, Courtesy* (London: Khaniqahi-Nimatullahi Publications, 1988).

For the importance of ethical behavior and the personal development of virtue in al-Ghazālī's writings, see Mohamed Ahmed Sharif, *Ghazali's Theory of Virtue* (Albany: State University of New York Press, 1975); and Muḥammad Abul Quasem, *The Ethics of al-Ghazālī: A Composite Ethics in Islam* (Selangor, Malaysia: Published by the author, 1976).

27. Translated by McCarthy in *Freedom and Fulfillment,* 89–90. Square brackets are the translator's.

28. Ibid., 92–93.

29. See Watt, "A Forgery in al-Ghazālī's *Mishkāt?*" *Journal of the Royal Asiatic Society of Great Britain and Ireland* 1949: 5–22. See also his "The Authenticity of the Works Attributed to al-Ghazālī," *Journal of the Royal Asiatic Society of Great Britain and Ireland* 1952: 24–45.

30. See Lazarus-Yafeh, *Studies in al-Ghazzālī,* 282, and also 25, 42n. 35, and 336n. 39; al-Ghazālī, *Mishkāt al-anwār,* ed. ᶜAfīfī, 22, 27; and Herbert A. Davidson, *Alfarabi, Avicenna, and Averroës on Intellect: Their Cosmologies, Theories of the Active Intellect, and Theories of Human Intellect* (New York: Oxford University Press, 1992), 134–35n. 53. Hermann Landolt provides the most convincing and penetrating critique of Watt's assertions; see his "Ghazālī and *'Religionswissenschaft,'*" 62–63 and passim.

31. See Wensinck, "Ghazālī's *Mishkāt,*" 212.

32. See Landolt, "Ghazālī and '*Religionswissenschaft*,'" 65–66, in which he references Fakhr al-Dīn Rāzī's multi-volume work *Al-tafsīr al-kabīr* (Cairo: n.p., A.H. 1354–1357 [1935–1938 C.E.]), 22:233–34; and the three-page text by Rāzī, "Risāla-yi Taʾwīlāt al-Ahādith al-Mushkila," in "Fakhr-i Rāzī va Mishkāt ul-Anvār-i Ghazzālī," by Nasrollah Pourjavady, *Maʿārif* 2 (A.H. 1364 [1945 C.E.]): 213–29. Landolt is not convinced that this Persian text is Rāzī's but feels confident that its discussion is "Rāzian" in nature and deals with *The Niche of Lights*. He contends that this short treatise was written by a disciple of Rāzī or by a member of his school (68, 71).

33. Ibid., 72.

34. See Gairdner, "Al-Ghazālī's *Mishkāt*," 133, which reproduces the relevant passage of the Arabic text of Ibn Rushd's *Al-kashf.*

35. Ibid., 138.

36. See Lazarus-Yafeh, *Studies in al-Ghazzālī*, 308.

37. See Gairdner's introduction to his translation of al-Ghazālī, *Mishkāt*, 18–19; and for an extended analysis of Ibn Rushd and Ibn Ṭufayl's criticisms, see Gairdner "Al-Ghazālī's *Mishkāt*," 133–54.

Landolt provides an excellent summary of these arguments and agrees that Ibn Rushd overstated his "emanationist" accusations against al-Ghazālī. Nevertheless, the question of al-Ghazālī's use of Neoplatonic ideas is not straightforward. Landolt argues that Ibn Rushd was justified, from a certain point of view, in accusing al-Ghazālī of such notions and shows that al-Ghazālī's distinction between *al-muṭāʿ* and God is the same as Ibn Sīnā's "distinction between the cause of universal motion and the cause of existence itself" ("Ghazālī and '*Religionswissenschaft*,'" 53–54). See also note 40 below.

38. See Davidson, *Alfarabi, Avicenna, and Averroës on Intellect*, 135.

39. Ibid., 136.

40. See also notes 30 and 37. For an analysis of the relationship of the *Mishkāt* to the theories of Ibn Sīnā, see ibid., 130–44. Davidson concludes his discussion by saying, "We find in the *Mishkat al-Anwar* [that] . . . Ghazali is not rejecting the structure of the universe depicted by Avicenna [Ibn Sīnā] or even the possibility that God produces everything outside himself through a series of emanations. He is merely rejecting Avicenna's explanation of the process" (153).

41. The relevant Arabic passage of *Ḥayy ibn Yaqẓān* and its English translation have been reproduced in Gairdner, "Al-Ghazālī's *Mishkāt*," 146.

42. Ibid., 145–51.

43. See Gairdner's introduction to his translation of al-Ghazālī, *Mishkāt*, 24.

44. See R. Nicholson, *The Idea of Personality in Sufism* (Lahore, Pakistan: Sh. Muḥammad Ashraf, 1970), 42–43.

45. See R. C. Zaehner, *Hindu and Muslim Mysticism* (London: Anthone Press, 1960), 173. Zaehner bases his conclusion on a passage in al-Ghazālī's *Fayṣal al-tafriqa bayn al-islām wa al-zandaqa* in which the angel Gabriel is given different names depending on the angel's relationship to God and others in the cosmos. Al-Ghazālī says that the name "one who is obeyed" is given to Gabriel "with respect to his being followed on the part of some of the Angels." See "Appendix I: *Fayṣal al-Tafriqa bayn al-Islām wa l-Zandaqa*," in McCarthy, *Freedom*

and Fulfillment, 155; and al-Ghazālī, *Fayṣal al-tafriqa,* in *Al-Quṣūr al-ᶜawālī,* ed. Muḥammad Muṣṭafa Abū al-ᶜAlī (Cairo: Dār al-Tabāᶜa al-Muḥammadiya, 1970), 1:134–35.

According to Zaehner, the word *muṭāᶜ* is mentioned once in the Qurᵓān (81:21) and the commentators equate it with Gabriel (*Hindu and Muslim Mysticism,* 173).

46. See Gairdner's introduction to his translation of al-Ghazālī, *Mishkāt,* 25; and Wensinck, "Ghazālī's *Mishkāt,*" 212.

47. See Wensinck, "Ghazālī's *Mishkāt,*" 211.

48. See Davidson, *Alfarabi, Avicenna, and Averroës on Intellect,* 135.

49. Ibid., n. 15.

50. See Lazarus-Yafeh, *Studies in al-Ghazzālī,* 349–411.

51. Ibid., 362.

52. This translation of the *Mīzān al-ᶜamal* is from ibid., 361. I have not seen the Arabic text. See also Gairdner's introduction to his translation of al-Ghazālī, *Mishkāt,* 19.

53. Discussions of the cosmology and psychology of al-Ghazālī have remained introductory. For example, Wensinck's "Ghazālī's Cosmology and Mysticism" mentions the Qurᵓānic, *ḥadīth,* and philosophical sources of al-Ghazālī's cosmological descriptions and presents a basic trilevel picture of the Islamic universe—the visible world *(shahāda),* the world of dominion *(malakūt),* and the world of power *(jabarūt).* An appendix entitled "Some Notes on al-Ghazālī's Cosmology" in Lazarus-Yafeh's *Studies in al-Ghazzālī* adds to Wensinck's analysis in that Lazarus-Yafeh is sensitive to al-Ghazālī's linguistic style. Hence, she points out important concepts missed by Wensinck, such as the innate connection between cosmology and psychology in the soul's search for God. But, as she herself admits, her analysis is preliminary. See also K. Nakamura, "Imām Ghazālī's Cosmology Reconsidered with Special Reference to the Concept *Jabarūt,*" *Studia Islamica* 80 (1994): 29–46.

54. Wensinck compares passages of *The Niche of Lights* to passages in Plotinus's *Enneads* and works of other Greek, Christian, and Jewish thinkers such as Philo, Stephen bar Sudaile, Isaac of Nineveh, Bar Hebraeus, and Goethe in light of their similar understanding of Neoplatonic thought. See Wensinck, "Ghazālī's *Mishkāt,*" 192–212.

55. See H. Wehr, *A Dictionary of Modern Written Arabic,* ed. J. Milton Cowan, 3d ed. (Ithaca, New York: Spoken Language Services, 1976), 1055; and D. B. Macdonald, "Tawḥīd," in *E. J. Brill's First Encyclopaedia of Islam, 1913–1936* (New York: E. J. Brill, 1987) 8:704.

56. See S. H. Nasr, *Science and Civilization in Islam,* 2d ed. (Cambridge: Islamic Texts Society, 1987), 21–22; and his work *An Introduction to Islamic Cosmological Doctrines,* rev. ed. (Boulder, Colorado: Shambala, 1978), 3–5.

57. For a summary of the idea of light in the works of al-Ghazālī, see "Chapter IV: Symbolism of Light in Al-Ghazzālī's Writings," in Lazarus-Yafeh, *Studies in al-Ghazzālī,* 264–348.

58. This is a common understanding in Islamic cosmology. See the sections "Qualitative Correspondence" and "Qualitative Levels" in Murata, *Tao of Islam,* 27–32.

59. See "Appendix II: Ghazālī on *Fanā'*, Annihilation of Self or Absorption in God," in Abd al-Raḥmān Jāmī, *Lawā'iḥ: A Treatise on Ṣūfism,* trans. E. H. Whinfield and Mirza Muḥammad Kazvini (Lahore, Pakistan: Islamic Book Foundation, 1978), 59–61.

60. See al-Ghazālī, *Le tabernacle des lumières (Michkāt al-anwār),* trans. Roger Deladrière (Paris: Editions du Seuil, 1981); *Die Nische der Lichter: Miskāt al-anwār,* trans. and ed. ʿAbd-Elsamad ʿAbd-Elhamīd Elschazlī, Philosophische Bibliothek Band 390 (Hamburg: Felix Meiner Verlag, 1987); Gairdner's translation of *Mishkāt;* and Laura Veccia Vaglieri and Robert Rubinacci, *Scritti scelti di al-Ghazālī a cura di L.V. V e R.R.6,* 563–614, as cited by Landolt, "Ghazālī and *'Religionswissenschaft,'*" 21n. 9.

[Author's Introduction]

1. This *ḥadīth* is mentioned twice in al-Ghazālī's *Revivification of the Religious Sciences,* but without the word "darkness." See al-Ghazālī, *Iḥyā',* 1:149, 504. Wensinck's *Concordance,* 1:424, has a similar *ḥadīth* which states "His veil is light" in place of "God has . . . darkness."

2. A Ṣūfī maxim.

3. Carl W. Ernst discusses the expression "to divulge the mystery of Lordship" in his analysis of the life and sayings of al-Ḥallāj (d. 922) and ʿAyn al-Quḍāt Hamadānī (d. 1131), two well-known Ṣūfīs put to death by the ruling authorities because of their ecstatic utterances *(shaṭḥīyāt)* on the nature of God, which were considered "unbelief" by those in power at that time. See Ernst's *Words of Ecstasy in Sufism* (Albany: State University of New York Press, 1985), 130–32.

4. This *ḥadīth* is not in Wensinck's *Concordance.* However, it is found twice in al-Ghazālī, *Iḥyā',* 1:33, 147. The longer version on page 33 adds: "Do not despise one who possesses knowledge which God has bestowed upon him, because God did not despise him when He bestowed it." See also al-Ghazālī, *The Book of Knowledge: Being a Translation with Notes of* The Kitāb al-ʿIlm *of Al-Ghazzālī's* Iḥyā' ʿUlūm al-Dīn, trans. Nabih Amin Faris (Lahore, Pakistan: Sh. Muḥammad Ashraf, 1962), 49.

5. Allusion to Qur'ān 94:1: "Did We not open up your breast for you?"

6. Al-Ghazālī attributes this saying, in two slightly different forms, to Jesus Christ in the *Iḥyā',* 1:56–57.

The First Chapter

1. Al-Ghazālī uses the term "light of the eye" to describe the eye's power to see.

2. This is a sound *ḥadīth* (see Wensinck, *Concordance,* 2:71).

3. See al-Ghazālī, *Iḥyā',* 3:7–74. A partial English translation of *A Book Setting Forth the Wonders of the Heart* is provided in Appendix V of al-Ghazālī, *Freedom and Fulfilment,* 363–82.

4. This *ḥadīth* is not found in Wensinck's *Concordance* and is not listed in the *ḥadīth* index of al-Ghazālī's *Iḥyā'*.

5. This is in reference to Qur᾽ān 3:30: "The day every soul shall find what it has done of good brought forward, and what it has done of evil."

6. The term "dominion" *(malakūt)* is derived from the Qur᾽ān (6:75; 7:185; 23:88; 36:83).

7. An allusion to Qur᾽ān 14:48: "Upon the day the earth shall be changed to other than the earth, and the heavens, and they sally forth unto God, the One, the Overwhelming."

8. This is an allusion to Qur᾽ān 95:4–5: "We indeed created man in the fairest stature, then We reduced him to the lowest of the low."

9. This is a variation of a sound *ḥadīth* (see Tirmīdhī, Imān, 18 and Aḥmad 2:176) that reads, "God created His creatures in darkness, then cast to them something of His light."

10. This *ḥadīth* is neither mentioned in Wensinck's *Concordance* nor listed in the *ḥadīth* index of al-Ghazālī's *Iḥyā᾽*.

11. This is in reference to the Qur᾽ānic version of Moses' encounter with God through the burning bush on Mount Sinai.

12. This is an allusion to Qur᾽ān 37:164–66: "None of us is there, but has a known station; we are those ranged in ranks, we are they that give glory."

13. "Those brought near to God" *(al-muqarrabūn)* is a title that the Qur᾽ān (4:172) gives to the angels.

14. For a discussion of the role and meaning of angels in Islamic cosmology, see Sachiko Murata, "Angels," in *Islamic Spirituality: Foundations,* ed. S. H. Nasr (New York: Crossroads, 1987).

15. *Ma*ᶜ*īya,* literally "with-ness," is a term derived from Qur᾽ān 57:4: "He is with you wherever you are."

16. For an English translation of this book by Burrell and Daher, see al-Ghazālī, *The Ninety-Nine Beautiful Names of God*, trans. D. Burrell and N. Daher (Cambridge: Islamic Texts Society, 1993).

17. These are famous ecstatic utterances, the first by al-Ḥallāj (d. 922) and the next two by Abū Yazīd Basṭāmī (d. 875). See Ernst, *Words of Ecstasy,* 3, 11, and passim.

18. "Unification" implies the uniting of two things and is normally condemned as a heresy in Islamic thought when it is used to explain the relationship between God and His creation. See Chittick and Wilson's discussion of "unificationism" in Fakhruddin ᶜIraqi, *Divine Flashes,* trans. and ed. William C. Chittick and Peter Lamborn Wilson (New York: Paulist Press, 1982), 145–46.

19. The "lover" here is al-Ḥallāj, and this is one-half of a line of a famous poem by him.

20. This oft-quoted poem is by Ṣāḥib ibn ᶜAbbād (d. 995). See ᶜIraqi, *Divine Flashes,* 82.

21. The descent to the heaven of this world is mentioned in a well-known *ḥadīth,* the text of which is as follows: "Our Lord descends to the heaven of this world every night and says, 'Is there any supplicator? Is there anyone asking for forgiveness?'" This *ḥadīth* is provided with minor variations in Muslim, Musāᶜrīn, 17 and Aḥmad 2:433 and 3:34.

22. Al-Ghazālī has already cited this as a *ḥadīth.*

23. This is a part of a sound *ḥadīth* (see Bukhārī, Riqāq, 38). A variation of

this *ḥadīth* reads as follows: "I love nothing that draws My servant near to Me more than [I love] what I have made obligatory for him. My servant never ceases drawing near to Me through supererogatory works until I love him. Then when I love him, I am his hearing through which he hears, his sight through which he sees, his hand through which he grasps, and his foot through which he walks." This translation is from Murata, *Tao of Islam,* 253.

24. The first part of the complete *ḥadīth* found in Muslim, Birr, 43, is as follows: "On the Day of Resurrection God will say, 'O son of Adam, I was ill and you did not visit Me.' He will reply, 'How should I visit Thee, when Thou art Lord of the worlds?' He will reply, 'Did you not know that my servant so-and-so was ill, but you did not visit him? Did you not know that had you visited him, you would have found Me with him?' " This translation is from William C. Chittick, *The Sufi Path of Knowledge: Ibn al-ʿArabī's Metaphysics of Imagination* (Albany: State University of New York Press, 1989), 392n. 33.

25. Allusion to four Qurʾānic verses: "Surely your Lord is God, who created the heavens and the earth in six days, and then sat Himself upon the Throne, governing the affair" (10:3); "He governs the affair from heaven to earth" (32:5); and also 10:31 and 13:2. Thus, according to al-Ghazālī's interpretation *(taʾwīl)* of this verse, the perfected seeker governs the levels of his own inner world just as God governs the heavens and the earth—or, rather, his governing himself in this state of singularity is identical with God governing himself.

26. According to Ibn al-ʿArabī (d. 1240), this saying belongs to the Prophet's relative through marriage and first political and religious successor—the first of the four "rightly guided" caliphs—Abū Bakr (d. 634). See Chittick, *Sufi Path of Knowledge,* 102, 178, 215, 348.

27. Because of Abū Bakr's piety he acquired the surname al-Ṣiddīq, "the Righteous," during the Prophet's lifetime.

28. This is a sound *ḥadīth*. See Chittick, *Faith and Practice,* 213, which lists Bukhārī, Tafsīr Sūra, 92, 93; Bukhārī, Adab, 120; Bukhārī, Qadar, 4; Bukhārī, Tawḥīd, 54; and Muslim, Qadar, 6–8.

The Second Chapter

1. See note 6 of the First Chapter. The term "kingdom" *(mulk)* is Qurʾānic (43:85; 45:27; 57:2; 67:1; 85:9).

2. Ismāʿīl ibn ʿUmar ibn Kathīr's Qurʾānic commentary states that the question was, "Trace the lineage of your Lord for us!" *(unsub lanā rabbaka).* See his *Tafsīr al-Qurʾān al-ʿaẓīm* (Beirut: Dār al-Jīl, 1990), 4:570.

3. Reference to the *ḥadīth,* "The veridical dream is one forty-sixth part of prophecy." See Wensinck, *Concordance,* 1:343.

4. The interpretation is by Ibn Sīrīn. See al-Ghazālī, *Iḥyāʾ* 4:362, and the English translation in *Remembrance of Death and Afterlife,* 153.

5. An allusion to Qurʾān 20:12, in which God commands Moses through the burning bush on Mount Sinai: "I am thy Lord; doff thy two sandals; thou art in the holy riverbed, Towa."

6. Al-Ghazālī's distinction here remains somewhat unclear. In paragraphs 33–34 of this chapter he presents his thoughts on the difference between the

presence of divinity, kingship, and lordship, so he probably had well-considered reasons for making the present distinction which a blind guess would not illuminate. An adequate answer would entail a complete perusal of al-Ghazālī's extant writings on this topic, assuming that he explained or even mentioned this matter anywhere else.

7. An allusion to a well-known prophetic saying, which is not accepted by the specialists: "He who knows himself knows his Lord." See Chittick, *Sufi Path of Knowledge,* 396n. 22.

8. The "All-Merciful" version is not found in the standard sources. In the instances where al-Ghazālī quotes this *ḥadīth* in the *Iḥyāʾ,* he employs the standard version, "in His form." Chittick, quoting Ibn al-ʿArabī, says, "Though this [the All-Merciful] version is not accepted by the authorities in the transmission of the *ḥadīth (aṣḥāb al-naql),* 'it has been shown to be sound *(ṣaḥīḥ)* by unveiling *(kashf)*'" (*Sufi Path of Knowledge,* 399–400n. 4). The word "sound" *(ṣaḥiḥ)* is a technical term used by scholars of *ḥadīth* to indicate that a *ḥadīth* is of reliable origin and not questionable—in which case the term "weak" *(ḍaʿīf)* is used.

9. See ibid., 412n. 5.

10. This is a sound *ḥadīth.* See Wensinck, *Concordance,* 6:52.

11. In a related passage in "Wonders of the Heart," al-Ghazālī says: "The pig is appetite, for a pig is not blameworthy because of its color, shape, and form, but because of its greed, burning thirst, and eager desire. The dog is anger, for the rapacious predator and the vicious dog are not 'dog' and 'predator' because of their form, color, and shape. The true meaning of 'predatoriness' is rapacity, animosity, and viciousness." Translation is from Murata, *Tao of Islam,* 258. See also al-Ghazālī, *Iḥyāʾ,* 3:9, and his *Freedom and Fulfillment,* 376–78.

12. An allusion to Qurʾān 7:20–25, in which the banishment of Adam and Eve from the Garden is brought about through Satan, who "leads astray through delusion" (7:22).

13. This is a sound *ḥadīth.* See Wensinck, *Concordance,* 1:416.

14. See note 3 above.

15. The other two branches seem to be knowledge of the sciences of unveiling (that is, knowledge of the objects of faith—God, the angels, the prophets, the Last Day, etc.) and the ability to perform miracles. See Chittick, *Faith and Practice,* 89.

16. Compare the following passage from al-Ghazālī, *Al-maqṣad al-asnā fī sharḥ maʿānī asmāʾ Allāh al-ḥusnā,* ed. Fadlou A. Shehadi (Beirut: Dar al-Machreq, 1971), 134–36: "Just as an infant in the cradle finds it difficult to understand the reality of discrimination, and the discriminating child finds it difficult to understand the reality of reason and the wonders that become unveiled in reason's stage before he reaches it, so also the stage of reason finds it difficult to understand the stages of friendship and prophecy." Translation is from Chittick, *Faith and Practice,* 194.

17. See paragraphs 32–33 of the First Chapter.

18. *Al-qusṭās al-mustaqīm.* Al-Ghazālī wrote this small treatise against a Bāṭinite's accusation that a Muslim must follow the Bāṭinite's hidden infallible teacher because true knowledge is impossible to ascertain without him.

19. This is a variation of a sound *ḥadīth* that reads, "Your love for a thing makes you blind and deaf." See Wensinck, *Concordance,* 1:409.

The Third Chapter

1. Gairdner and Landolt attempt to find Islamic and non-Islamic theological groupings that correspond to al-Ghazālī's classification, and some of their interpretations of those groups not explicitly named in the text are included in the notes that follow. Landolt provides a more thorough analysis than Gairdner, along with a great number of references to the texts of the thinkers he classifies. See Gairdner in the introduction to his translation of al-Ghazālī, *Mishkāt,* 9–14; and Landolt, "Ghazālī and *'Religionswissenschaft,'* " 31–52.

2. This *ḥadīth* is not found in Wensinck's *Concordance*, but it is mentioned twice in al-Ghazālī's *Iḥyā*ʾ, 1:52 and 4:458.

3. This list is suggested in the Qurʾānic reference to *ḥubb al-shahawāt,* "the love of objects of appetite" (3:14).

4. This is a sound *ḥadīth.* See Wensinck, *Concordance,* 1:283.

5. Landolt designates this group in general as polytheists. See his "Ghazālī and *'Religionswissenschaft,'* " 33.

6. Gairdner suggests that these are "the polytheists of Hellenic (? and Indian) type." See the introduction to his translation of al-Ghazālī, *Mishkāt,* 10.

7. Gairdner identifies this group as the fire worshippers or Magians; ibid.

8. These names refer to Zoroastrian religious beliefs. Yazdān is the principle of light, while Ahriman is its dark opposite. See V. F. Büchner, "Yazdān," in *E. J. Brill's First Encyclopedia of Islam, 1913–1936* (Leiden: E. J. Brill, 1987) 8:1161–62.

9. These are the monotheist "Corporealists," according to Landolt, "Ghazālī and *'Religionswissenschaft,'* " 33.

10. Literally, that which gives something a body *(jism)*: "The Mujassima, as indicated by their name, are those who maintain that God has a body" (Chittick, *Faith and Practice,* 194).

11. *Karrāmiya* was a name given to a sect which grew in the central and eastern parts of the Islamic world from the ninth century until the Mongol invasion. They followed the teachings of Abū ʿAbd Allah Muḥammad ibn Karrām (d. 868–69), whose doctrines included a belief "that God was a substance *(djawhar)* . . . and that He had a body *(djism)* finite in a certain direction when He comes into contact *(mumāssa)* with the throne, thus interpreting the much-discussed kurʾānic verse XX,5, *al-Raḥmān ʿalā 'l-ʿarsh istawā,* 'the Merciful One has sat down firmly on the throne . . . .' " (C. E. Bosworth, "Karrāmiyya," in *The Encyclopaedia of Islam,* new ed. (Leiden: E. J. Brill, 1978) 4:667–69; original spelling retained.)

12. Gairdner says that these are "extreme Ḥanbalites: Ẓāhirites"; but Landolt does not think Ḥanbalites belong in this category. See Landolt, "Ghazālī and *'Religionswissenschaft,'* " 35.

13. Landolt calls these the Muslim "Attributists." Ibid., 33. The first of these two groups is identified by Gairdner as "early literalists; Ḥanbalites;

early Ash^{c}arites." The second group is the "later Ash^{c}arites," according to him. See the introduction to his translation of al-Ghazālī, *Mishkāt,* 11–12.

14. Gairdner says that this refers to "Ḥasan al-Baṣrī, al-Shāfi^{c}ī, and others of the *bilā kaifa* school" (ibid., 12). Landolt adds early Mu^{c}tazila thought and certain philosophical teachings of the early Islamic philosopher al-Kindī. See his "Ghazālī and *'Religionswissenschaft,'*" 39.

15. Here al-Ghazālī is comparing the angelic "lord" of each type with the similitudes of light found in his previous discussion in paragraphs 11–15 of the Second Chapter. There he explained that the light of the stars, the moon, and the sun found in the Qurʾānic story of Abraham's search for his "lord" (Qurʾān 6:76–79) are similitudes of those angels encountered by Abraham in his journey. First Abraham viewed an angel whose similitude of light in this world is that of the stars. He took this angel to be his lord; but after realizing that this angel's light, like starlight, was deficient through setting, he knew it could not be his lord. So he climbed from that level to the level of an angel whose similitude of light in this world is moonlight. As before, this next angel's deficiency of light then prompted him to climb to the level of an even higher existent being whose light had the similitude of this world's sunlight. Finally, Abraham realized his previous mistakes and turned his face to the true Lord, who is the originator and source of all these lights. In al-Ghazālī's present discussion, the people who have reached this last mentioned level are called "those who have arrived" *(al-wāṣilūn).* But he goes on to indicate that even these people are divided into a heirarchy.

16. According to Gairdner in the introduction to his translation of al-Ghazālī's *Mishkāt,* these are the Ṣūfī philosophers and perhaps al-Fārābī (12).

17. According to Gairdner, these are also Ṣūfī philosophers and al-Ghazālī himself at an earlier point in his life; see the introduction to his translation of al-Ghazālī's *Mishkāt,* 13. Landolt argues that this third group consists of the Ismā^{c}īlīs; see his "Ghazālī and *'Religionswissenschaft,'*" 42–43.

18. *Al-wāṣilūn.* Al-Ghazālī mentions that Abraham and Muḥammad belong to this last group. Landolt in his "Ghazālī and *'Religionswissenschaft,'*" reserves this group for the Ṣūfīs and adds that "they are mystics in the Neoplatonic sense of the term—and in the sense in which Avicenna may be said to have been a mystic" (50).

19. See paragraphs 45–46 of the First Chapter.

20. Perhaps al-Ghazālī has in mind here the well-known "Night Journey" *(mi^{c}rāj)* of the Prophet in which, in a single night, Muḥammad journeyed through all the levels of created existence to God.

Bibliography

Translations of the works of al-Ghazālī and other medieval Arabic writers are listed under the author's name rather than the translator's.

Abul Quasem, Muḥammad. *The Ethics of al-Ghazālī: A Composite Ethics in Islam.* Selangor, Malaysia: Published by the author, 1976.

Arberry, Arthur J. *The Koran Interpreted.* New York: Macmillan, 1955.

Bosworth, C. E. "Karrāmiyya." In *The Encyclopaedia of Islam.* New ed. Vol. 4. Leiden: E. J. Brill, 1978.

Bouyges, P. *Essai de chronologie des oeuvres de al-Ghazali.* Edited by M. Allard. Beirut: n.p., 1959.

Brenner, Louis. "Concepts of Ṭarīqa in West Africa: The Case of the Qādiriyya." In *Charisma and Brotherhood in African Islam.* Edited by Donal B. Cruise O'Brien and Christian Coulon. Oxford: Clarendon Press, 1988.

Brockelmann, Carl, and L. Gardet. "Al-Djuwaynī, Abu 'l-Maᶜālī ᶜAbd al-Malik." In *The Encyclopaedia of Islam.* New ed. Vol. 2. Leiden: E. J. Brill, 1965.

Büchner, V. F. "Yazdān." In *E. J. Brill's First Encyclopedia of Islam, 1913–1936.* Vol. 8. Leiden: E. J. Brill, 1987.

Chittick, William C. "Dhikr." In *Encyclopedia of Religion.* Vol 4. New York: Macmillan, 1987.

———. *Faith and Practice of Islam: Three Thirteenth Century Sufi Texts.* Albany: State University of New York Press, 1992.

———. *The Sufi Path of Knowledge: Ibn al-ᶜArabī's Metaphysics of Imagination.* Albany: State University of New York Press, 1989.

Davidson, Herbert A. *Alfarabi, Avicenna, and Averroës on Intellect: Their Cosmologies, Theories of the Active Intellect, and Theories of Human Intellect.* New York: Oxford University Press, 1992.

Ernst, Carl W. *Words of Ecstasy in Sufism.* Albany: State University of New York Press, 1985.

Fakhry, Majid. *A History of Islamic Philosophy.* 2d ed. New York: Columbia University Press, 1983.

Gairdner, W. H. T. "Al-Ghazālī's *Mishkāt al-Anwār* and the Ghazālī Problem." *Der Islam* 5 (1914): 121–53.

Gardner, W. R. W. *An Account of al-Ghazālī's Life and Works.* Madras: n.p., 1919.

Al-Ghazālī, Abū Ḥāmid. *The Book of Knowledge: Being a Translation with Notes of* The Kitāb al-ᶜIlm *of Al-Ghazzālī's* Iḥyāᵓ ᶜUlūm al-Dīn. Translated by Nabih Amin Faris. Lahore, Pakistan: Sh. Muḥammad Ashraf, 1962.

———. *Die Nische der Lichter: Miskāt al-anwār.* Translated and edited by ᶜAbd-Elsamad ᶜAbd-Elhamīd Elschazlī. Philosophische Bibliothek Band 390. Hamburg: Felix Meiner Verlag, 1987.

———. *Fayṣal al-tafriqa.* In *Al-Quṣūr al-ᶜawālī.* Edited by Muḥammad Muṣṭafa Abū al-ᶜAlī. Vol. 1. Cairo: Dār al-Tabāᶜa al-Muḥammadiya, 1970.

———. *Freedom and Fulfillment: An Annotated Translation of al-Ghazālī's* Al-Munqidh min al-Dalāl *and Other Relevant Works of al-Ghazālī.* Translated by Richard Joseph McCarthy. Boston: Twayne, 1980.

———. *Al-Ghazālī on Divine Predicates and Their Properties: A Critical and Annotated Translation of These Chapters in* Al-Iqtiṣād fil-Iᶜtiqād. Translated by ᶜAbdu-r-rahmān Abū Zayd. 1970. Reprint, Lahore, Pakistan: Sh. Muḥammad Ashraf, 1974.

———. *Iḥyāᵓ ᶜulūm al-dīn* (The revivification of the religious sciences). 5 vols. Beirut: Dār al-Hādī, 1992.

———. *The Incoherence of the Philosophers.* Translated by Michael E. Marmura. Islamic Translation Series. Provo, Utah: Brigham Young University Press, 1997.

———. *Invocations and Supplications: Kitāb al-Adhkār wa 'l-Daᶜawāt, Book IX of* The Revival of the Religious Sciences, Iḥyāᵓ ᶜUlūm al-Dīn. Translated by K. Nakamura. Rev. ed. Cambridge: Islamic Texts Society, 1990. Originally published as *Ghazālī on Prayer,* Tokyo: University of Tokyo, 1973.

———. *Le tabernacle des lumières (Michkāt al-anwār).* Translated by Roger Deladrière. Paris: Editions du Seuil, 1981.

———. *Al-maqṣad al-asnā fī sharḥ maᶜānī asmāᵓ Allāh al-ḥusnā.* Edited by Fadlou A. Shehadi. Beirut: Dar al-Machreq, 1971.

———. *Mishkāt al-anwār.* Edited by Abū al-ᶜAlā ᶜAfīfī. Cairo: Al-Dār al-Qawmīya lil-Tabāᶜa wa al-Nashar, 1964.

———. *Mishkāt al-Anwār (The Niche for Lights).* Translated by W. H. T. Gairdner. 1924. Reprint, Lahore, Pakistan: Sh. Muḥammad Ashraf, 1952.

———. *The Ninety-Nine Beautiful Names of God.* Translated by D. Burrell and N. Daher. Cambridge: Islamic Texts Society, 1993.

———. *The Precious Pearl: A Translation from the Arabic, with Notes, of the* Kitāb al-Durra al-Fākhira fī Kashf ᶜUlūm al-Ākhira *of Abū Ḥāmid Muḥammad b. Muḥammad b. Muḥammad al-Ghazālī.* Translated and edited by Jane Idleman Smith. Harvard University Studies in World Religion, no. 1. Missoula, Montana: Scholars Press, 1979.

———. *The Remembrance of Death and the Afterlife (Kitāb Dhikr al-Mawt wa-Mā Baᶜduhu), Book XL of* The Revival of the Religious Sciences, Iḥyāᵓ ᶜUlūm al-Dīn. Translated by T. J. Winter. Cambridge: Islamic Texts Society, 1989.

Al-Ghazālī, Aḥmad. *Sawānih: Inspirations from the World of Pure Spirits: The Oldest Persian Sufi Treatise on Love.* Translated by Nasrollah Pourjavady. London: KPI, 1986.

Hodgson, M. G. S. "Bāṭinīya." In *The Encyclopaedia of Islam.* New ed. Vol. 1. Leiden: E. J. Brill, 1960.

Hourani, G. F. "The Chronology of Ghazālī's Writing." *Journal of the American Oriental Society* 89 (1959): 225–33.

Ibn Kathīr, Ismāʿīl ibn ʿUmar. *Tafsīr al-Qurʾān al-ʿazīm.* Beirut: Dār al-Jīl, 1990.

Ibn Rushd. *Averroës'* Tahafut al-Tahafut. Translated by S. van den Bergh. London: n.p., 1954.

ʿIraqi, Fakhruddin. *Divine Flashes.* Translated and edited by William C. Chittick and Peter Lamborn Wilson. New York: Paulist Press, 1982.

Jāmī, Abd al-Raḥmān. *Lawāʾiḥ: A Treatise on Ṣūfism.* Translated by E. H. Whinfield and Mirza Muḥammad Kazvini. Lahore, Pakistan: Islamic Book Foundation, 1978.

Landolt, Hermann. "Ghazālī and *'Religionswissenschaft'*: Some Notes on the *Mishkāt al-Anwār* for Professor Charles J. Adams." *Asiatische Studien (Etudes asiatiques)* 45, no. 1 (1991): 1–72.

Lazarus-Yafeh, Hava. *Studies in al-Ghazzālī.* Jerusalem: Magnes Press, 1975.

Macdonald, D. B. "The Life of al-Ghazzālī, with Especial Reference to His Religious Experiences and Opinions." *Journal of the American Oriental Society* 20 (1899): 71–132.

———. "Tawḥīd." In *E. J. Brill's First Encyclopaedia of Islam, 1913–1936.* Vol. 8. New York: E. J. Brill, 1987.

Murata, Sachiko. "Angels." In *Islamic Spirituality: Foundations.* Edited by S. H. Nasr. New York: Crossroads, 1987.

———. *The Tao of Islam: A Sourcebook on Gender Relationships in Islamic Thought.* Albany: State University of New York Press, 1992.

Murata, Sachiko, and William C. Chittick. *The Vision of Islam.* New York: Paragon House, 1994.

Nakamura, K., "Imām Ghazālī's Cosmology Reconsidered with Special Reference to the Concept *Jabarūt.*" *Studia Islamica* 80 (1994): 29–46.

Nasr, S. H. *An Introduction to Islamic Cosmological Doctrines.* Rev. ed. Boulder, Colorado: Shambala, 1978.

———. *Science and Civilization in Islam.* 2d ed. Cambridge: Islamic Texts Society, 1987.

Nicholson, R. *The Idea of Personality in Sufism.* Lahore, Pakistan: Sh. Muḥammad Ashraf, 1970.

Nurbakhsh, Javad, ed. *Sufism IV: Repentance, Abstinence, Renunciation, Wariness, Humility, Humbleness, Sincerity, Constancy, Courtesy.* London: Khaniqahi-Nimatullahi Publications, 1988.

Rāzī, Fakhr al-Dīn. *Al-tafsīr al-kabīr.* Cairo: n.p., A.H. 1354–1357 [1935–1938 C.E.]. Quoted in Herman Landolt, "Ghazālī and *'Religionswissenschaft,'*" q.v.

———. "Risāla-yi Taʾwīlāt al-Ahādith al-Mushkila." In "Fakhr-i Rāzī va Mishkāt ul-Anvār-i Ghazzālī," by Nasrollah Pourjavady. *Maʿārif* 2 (A.H. 1364 [1945 C.E.]): 213–29. Quoted in Herman Landolt, "Ghazālī and *'Religionswissenschaft,'*" q.v.

Ritter, H. "Al-Ghazālī, Aḥmad B. Muḥammad." In *The Encyclopaedia of Islam.* New ed. Vol 2. Leiden: E. J. Brill, 1965.

Saeed Sheikh, M. "Al-Ghazālī." In *A History of Muslim Philosophy: With Short Accounts of Other Disciplines and the Modern Renaissance in Muslim Lands.* Edited by M. M. Sharif. Vol. 1. Wiesbaden: Otto Harrassowitz, 1963.

Schimmel, Annemarie. *Mystical Dimensions of Islam.* Chapel Hill: University of North Carolina Press, 1975.

Sharif, Mohamed Ahmed. *Ghazali's Theory of Virtue.* Albany: State University of New York Press, 1975.

Siddīqi, M. A. *Ḥadīth Literature: Its Origin, Development, and Special Features.* Cambridge: Islamic Texts Society, 1993.

Smith, Margaret. *Al-Ghazālī the Mystic.* 1944. Reprint, Lahore, Pakistan: Hijra International, 1983.

Vaglieri, Laura Veccia, and Robert Rubinacci. *Scritti scelti di al-Ghazālī a cura di L.V.V. e R.R.* Turin: Unione Tipigrafico, 1970. Quoted in Herman Landolt, "Ghazālī and *'Religionswissenschaft,'*" q.v.

Watt, W. Montgomery. "The Authenticity of the Works Attributed to al-Ghazālī." *Journal of the Royal Asiatic Society of Great Britain and Ireland* (1952): 24–45.

———. *The Faith and Practice of al-Ghazālī.* London: G. Allen and Unwin, 1953.

———. "A Forgery in al-Ghazālī's *Mishkāt?*" *Journal of the Royal Asiatic Society of Great Britain and Ireland* (1949): 5–22.

———. "Al-Ghazālī, Abū Ḥāmid Muḥammad b. Muḥammad al-Ṭūsī." In *The Encyclopedia of Islam.* New ed. Vol. 2. Leiden: E. J. Brill, 1965.

———. "Al-Ghazālī, Abū Ḥāmid." *The Encyclopedia of Religion.* Vol. 5. New York: Macmillan, 1987.

———. *Islamic Philosophy and Theology.* Edinburgh: Edinburgh University Press, 1962.

———. *Muslim Intellectual: A Study of al-Ghazālī.* Edinburgh: Edinburgh University Press, 1963.

Wehr, H. *A Dictionary of Modern Written Arabic.* Edited by J. Milton Cowan. 3d ed. Ithaca, New York: Spoken Language Services, 1976.

Wensinck, A. J. *Concordance et indices de la tradition musulmane.* 2d ed. 8 vols. Leiden: E. J. Brill, 1992.

———. "Ghazālī's *Mishkāt al-Anwār (Niche of Lights)*" In *Semietische Studien: Uit de Nalatenschap.* Leiden: A. W. Sijthoff's Uitgeversmaatschappij N.V., 1941.

———. "On the Relation between Ghazālī's Cosmology and His Mysticism." Mededeelingen der koninklijke Akademie van Wetenschappen, Afdeeling Letterkunde 75 (series A), no. 6 (1933):183–209.

Woodward, Mark. *Islam in Java: Normative Piety and Mysticism in the Sultanate of Yogyakarta.* Tucson: University of Arizona Press, 1989.

Zaehner, R. C. *Hindu and Muslim Mysticism.* London: Anthone Press, 1960.

Zwemer, Samuel. *A Moslem Seeker after God: Showing Islam at Its Best in the Life and Teaching of al-Ghazali, Mystic and Theologian of the Eleventh Century.* New York: Fleming H. Revell, 1920.

Index of Qurʾānic Verses

Index of *Ḥadīths* and Sayings

Index of Names and Terms

About the Translator

DAVID BUCHMAN was awarded a Ph.D. in sociocultural anthropology at the State University of New York at Stony Brook, where he received his master's degree. For his dissertation he completed two years of field research on the beliefs and practices of a Ṣūfī order in Yemen. As a Stony Brook undergraduate, he majored in religious studies with an emphasis on Islam. He has traveled throughout the Middle East pursuing the study of Arabic, Islam, and the status of contemporary Ṣūfism. He is currently an assistant professor of anthropology and Middle East studies at Hanover College in Indiana.

A Note on the Type

The English text of this book was set in BASKERVILLE, a typeface originally designed by John Baskerville (1706–1775), a British stonecutter, letter designer, typefounder, and printer. The Baskerville type is considered to be one of the first "transitional" faces—a deliberate move away from the "old style" of the Continental humanist printer. Its rounded letterforms presented a greater differentiation of thick and thin strokes, the serifs on the lower-case letters were more nearly horizontal, and the stress was nearer the vertical—all of which would later influence the "modern" style undertaken by Bodoni and Didot in the 1790s. Because of its high readability, particularly in long texts, the type was subsequently copied by all major typefoundries. (The original punches and matrices still survive today at Cambridge University Press.) This adaptation of Baskerville, designed by the Compugraphic Corporation in the 1960s, is a notable departure from other versions in its overall typographic evenness and lightness in color. To enhance its range, supplemental diacritics and ligatures were created in 1997 for exclusive use in the Islamic Translation Series.

TYPOGRAPHY BY JONATHAN SALTZMAN

◆